Trout Tactics

A Comprehensive Guide For The Conventional Tackle Angler

By Cal Kellogg

Author: Cal Kellogg
All photos except where noted: Copyright © 2013 Cal Kellogg
Cover Illustration / Design: Greg Bilbo

Library of Congress Control Number: 2013957600
Library of Congress subject headings suggestions:
1. GV191.2-200.66 Outdoor life - Outdoor recreation
2. SK650-664 Wildlife-related recreation

BIASC / BASIC Classification Suggestions:
1. SPO022000 SPORTS & RECREATION / Fishing
3. SPO030000 SPORTS & RECREATION / Outdoor Skills
4. SEL021000 SELF-HELP / Motivational & Inspirational

ISBN-13 for Black and White Version: 978-1-937355-09-8   V: 1.0

To purchase additional copies of *Trout Tactics* or to learn more about the author go to his website: www.fishsniffer.com

Big Mac Publisher Book Titles may be purchased in bulk at great discounts. Contact Cal Kellogg, or go to Big Mac Publisher's website. www.bigmacpublishers.com

Published By Big Mac Publishers for Kellogg Outdoors (530) 320-0368
Printed and bound in the United States of America

Trout Tactics

Quotes from well-respected trout anglers.

"*Trout Tactics* is the most comprehensive trout fishing book available to date -- bar none." **–Paul Kneeland, Publisher Fish Sniffer Magazine.**

"Cal's body of knowledge when it comes to trout fishing is impressive. Reading *Trout Tactics* will make you a better trout angler." **–Burt Carey, National Wild Turkey Federation.**

"Reading Cal's book changed the way I fish for trout. I carry a copy of it with me in my boat." **–Ross King, Sacramento, Ca.**

"If you're a trout angler, *Trout Tactics* is a must have reference." **Scott George, Denver, Co.**

"*Trout Tactics* is a must own book for everyone that targets trout with spinning and trolling gear." **–Tom Chen, San Francisco, Ca.**

Dedication

This book is dedicated to the trout anglers:

They hunt the cool water and enthusiastically embrace the challenge of high mountain cold, wind, white caps, rain, snow and even blistering sun, all in an effort to feel the intoxicating power of hard charging trout...

Table Of Contents

***

Acknowledgements

A lot of folks stepped up and gave me a helping hand on this project and I owe them all a profound debt of gratitude.

My wife Gena helped me tremendously both in the field and in the office gathering and editing material for this volume. A decade ago she supported my decision to become a full-time outdoor writer...Thanks Gena!

Of course my folks, Calvin and Claire Kellogg deserve a special thanks. Both are great trout anglers and they got me started on the path to trout fishing success at an early age...Thanks Mom and Dad!

A special thanks goes out to all the folks at Team Fish Sniffer including Dan Bacher, Paul Kneeland, Sheldon Bright, Ernie Marlan, Danny Lloyd, Wes Ward and Brooke Cyphers. Surrounded by a crew of such talented and creative folks like you, it's hard *not* to achieve great things...Thanks Team Fish Sniffer!

Last but not least I'd like to thank everyone that provided photos for this project including. Paul Kneeland, Dan Bacher, Rick Kennedy, Jason Thatcher, Gene St. Denis, Monte Smith, Bruce Wicks and Dave Barsi.

Cal Kellogg - Addicted trout angler!

Foreword

This Isn't One Of Those Fancy Fly Fishing Books

As long time editors of the Fish Sniffer Magazine hardly a week goes by when Dan Bacher and I don't receive a copy of the latest and greatest fly-fishing book available for review in the mail.

Most of these books are not only exceptionally well written, but they are also works of art. Such books are printed on the finest high gloss stock and are bristling with full color photos of exceptional quality.

I know how to produce a book like this, but what I don't know how to do is produce a book that exhibits such a high level of artistry while maintaining a realistic price point. Publishing costs are through the roof. And let's face it, the average Joe trout angler out there isn't going to shell out $50 for a book no matter how good the content is.

Luckily for me, when I set out to produce the book you are currently reading, "Trout Tactics" I wasn't trying to create art. I was out to produce the most definitive guide to conventional tackle trout fishing available and I wanted to have a finished product that sold at a realistic price. I think I've achieved both goals by a wide margin.

Bank fishing with bait and lures, trolling, using natural baits, lure selection and presentation, tackle considerations, targeting trophy trout, stream trout, weather effects and so much more, it's all covered in Trout Tactics.

I've been trout fishing on the West Coast since the '70's and I've been covering trout fishing with some of the finest guides available as a full time outdoor writer for nearly a decade. If it pertains to trout fishing, with the exception of fishing with fly tackle, you'll find it in this book!

It wasn't long after I joined the staff of the Fish Sniffer that I penned my first book, The Trout Fishing Handbook. That book was a hit with trout anglers residing up and down the West Coast and I sent plenty of them to the Great Lakes region as well.

Even though The Trout Fishing Handbook has been out of print for several years, I still get calls inquiring about buying a copy. It was these calls that prompted me to produce Trout Tactics.

All of the information presented in The Trout Fishing Handbook has been updated and is presented here. In addition I've added more than a dozen new chapters to cover advances and innovations I've learned since publishing The Trout Fishing Handbook.

The one area that is lacking in Trout Tactics comes in the form of photos. The more photos a book has the more expensive is it is to publish and it adds up fast. Everybody likes photos, but once again I had to compromise between what I'd like in a perfect world and a realistic price point.

The overriding thought in my mind as I put this project together was helping trout anglers catch more and bigger trout. If I had to throw photos under the bus to do that, so be it....

Along these lines, I have set up an ever-growing photo reference to accompany Trout Tactics on The Fish Sniffer Website. Simply type www.fishsniffer.com into your search engine, find the icon on the bottom of the home page that says, "Trout Tactics Photos" and start browsing!

Put what you learn from this book to work on the water and you'll achieve great results, whether you are a green beginner just getting started in the trout fishing scene or a seasoned veteran looking to hone your skills even more!

Email me photos of the trout you catch, your rigs and any feedback to trouttactics@fishsniffer.com. Cal Kellogg - 2013

Chapter One: Why Trout?

I've caught thousands of trout over the years, but I can still remember catching the first one as if it happened yesterday...

Despite the fact that it was late June the morning air was infused with the chill of the high Sierras and I could see my breath as I followed dad along the willow lined path. As we moved, I scanned the sandy ground for the heart shaped pockmarks that betrayed the movements of feeding deer the night before. A few hundred yards from our car the path rose slightly and the gurgle of the small creek became more intense. Presently we came to a small gravel bar that led down to a break in the streamside brush.

Dad walked down to the upstream side of the opening. "We'll hide behind these bushes, so the trout can't see us," dad said as he clamped a small split shot to the spinning rod's line and tied a small gold hook below it. After baiting the hook with a bright red salmon egg he flipped the rig into a riffle that flowed down into a small pool.

Almost immediately I saw the rod tip twitch a couple times and dad passed the rod to me. "Okay just let the bait set in that pool until you get a bite," he said. A few seconds later I felt some hard tugs and started reeling frantically as my heart raced. After I craned the feisty trout out of the water dad removed the hook. Before we put the fish in dad's creel he showed me its spots and explained that it was called a rainbow because of the red stripe running down its side.

Looking back I know that the trout had taken the bait before dad handed me the rod, but for a six year old it was pretty heady stuff. I've been hooked on trout fishing ever since.

If we consider the lower 48 states as a whole, black bass, bluegill and catfish are the most popular species among freshwater anglers by a solid margin. However, here on the west coast things are different. Sure black bass have a strong following in our neck of the woods, but when you get right down to it, trout are the reigning kings and why wouldn't they be?

The members of the trout family are sleek hard fighting gamefish that commonly grow to trophy proportions in our cold forage rich western waters. When I think of the trout I've known it's their physical power and regal beauty that springs to mind. Indeed, from the speckled majesty of a broad shouldered brown trout to the high country brook trout with its mottled green back fading away to a spectacular explosion of iridescent blue and red spots decorating its flank, there is no family of freshwater fish that possess the beauty of the trout.

In addition to their beauty, trout enjoy a broad distribution that few other west coast gamefish can match. Trout are at home in pristine high country streams, foothill reservoirs urban ponds and just about everywhere in between. As a result there are very few anglers here on the west coast that live more than a short drive from a productive trout fishery.

Undoubtedly, one of the most important factors driving the popularity of trout among anglers is the fact that they are willing strikers that can be caught all year long by fishermen using a variety of different techniques. I like to call trout equal opportunity gamefish because both bank and boat anglers achieve a high level of success while targeting them.

At the end of a long day on the water another important attribute of the trout family comes into play. I'm talking about the fine table fare that those trout residing in your cooler will provide. Trout are as delicious as they are handsome and can be prepared in a myriad of different ways. Whether you're preference is to drop them in a pan of sizzling bacon grease, roast them on the barbeque grill, bake them in a casserole dish or hang them in a smoker you're in for some good eating when all is said and done!

Up until now the vast majority of trout fishing books have focused on fly fishing techniques. In the following chapters we will thoroughly explore all aspects of catching trout here on the west coast using conventional gear. We're going to be talking about dodgers, downriggers, night crawlers, PowerBait and a whole lot more. If you're a fly guy you should stop reading, so your mind doesn't become corrupted with images of hard charging rainbows inhaling inflated worms or stately brown trout assaulting trolled plugs or worst of all, a beautifully tied fly pulsing behind a set of flashers. If you are a veteran conventional tackle angler prepare to learn some new approaches and techniques that will make you even more effective. If you are a greenhorn you'll garner a body of knowledge that would take years of trial and error experimentation to acquire.

Chapter Two: The Trout Lifestyle

This is a fishing book not a biology textbook, so I'm not going to bore you with a long complex description of the biology and physiology of trout that neither you nor I really understand. However, if your goal is to become a successful or more successful trout angler, having a basic understanding of the needs and behaviors of trout can only make you more effective out on the water. This being the case, let's take a look at the basics in terms of trout biology and behavior.

Trout have been swimming about the waters of North America since the last ice age. Trout as a species are defined as cold water fish because they are only found in lakes and streams that feature cool water with ample dissolved oxygen. The trout family boasts a long list of subspecies, but for our purposes I'm going to focus on the four species of trout most often targeted by trout anglers here on the west coast, these include rainbows, browns, mackinaw and brook trout.

Rainbow trout were originally found only in Pacific coast streams ranging as far north as Alaska and as far south as the Rio Santo Domingo River in Baja California. Rainbow trout are easily reared in hatcheries and adapt to new waters well. As a result rainbows have been widely planted and they are now the most widespread trout species in the world.

Rainbows sport a chrome colored flank with a bright red to pale pink colored band extending from the gill plate down the sides of the body near the lateral line. A rainbow's back is dark olive-blue and well dotted with black spots.

Temperatures in the 55 to 60 degree range are most comfortable for rainbows, but they can survive in water that is much colder than 55 and much warmer than 60.

Insects, baitfish, plankton, crustaceans and fish eggs all represent forage to rainbows. In general, stream dwelling rainbows feed mainly on insects while 'bows living in lakes and reservoirs survive mainly on a diet of baitfish. Yet, there are some streams and rivers that feature strong baitfish populations, which rainbows target readily. On the other hand there are many lakes, particularly at higher elevations that feature a forage base dominated by aquatic insects and of course rainbows in these lakes make their living eating bugs. On the average, stream trout run smaller than trout living in large rivers, lakes and reservoirs. This is primarily due to the fact that rainbows feeding on insects grow more slowly than those that dine on baitfish.

Rainbows spawn in streams during the springtime when the water temperature is between 50 and 60 degrees.

Rainbows spawn on gravel that features enough current to keep the eggs well oxygenated and free from silt and sediment.

Brown trout are not native to North America. Our browns originally came from Germany and Scotland. They were first introduced to North American waters in the 1800's. Browns have adapted well to this continent. Through natural migration and stocking programs browns have steadily increased their range.

The flanks of the brown trout are typically brownish or yellowish in color, but in lakes they can take on a silvery hue. Browns sport numerous black spots and generally display a few bright red or subtle orange spots along the lateral line. The coloration becomes dark on the back and fades to white on the belly. Young browns often have a slightly forked tail, while mature fish display a distinctly square tail. Browns prefer water that averages between 50 and 60 degrees just like rainbows do, but they show more adaptability to colder and warmer water temperatures.

Brown trout are favorites among trout anglers because they grow large and are challenging to hook consistently. Based on game department studies throughout the western United States, browns residing in lakes, reservoirs and large rivers average around 2 pounds and range up to and beyond 10 pounds. Browns in the 14 to 24 inch range are common.

Browns, particularly larger specimens put up a strong fight, but are not as likely as rainbows to put on an aerial display. The largest browns in most waters are nocturnal, doing most of their feeding between dusk and dawn. Small browns feed on a wide range of aquatic insects and minnows, but larger browns feed almost exclusively on other fish and crawfish. When big browns are on the feed they will also consume organisms such as frogs, birds, and mice that find themselves at the wrong place at the wrong time.

Brown trout like rainbows spawn in streams. But unlike 'bows, browns spawn in the fall and winter with the months from October through February seeing most of the spawning activity. Well oxygenated gravel beds represent the preferred location for spawning.

After spawning the female trout covers the eggs with gravel. The eggs lay virtually dormant through the winter months. In the spring the increasing length of daylight combined with rising water temperatures activates the eggs and prompts them to hatch.

While lake trout or mackinaw, as they are called in many areas of the country, are members of the salmonid family just like rainbows and browns, they are not a true trout. They are actually a char. Mackinaw are a mysterious fish that spend much of their time cruising in deep water.

Macks, while being extremely slow growing are long lived and capable of reaching massive proportions. Lakers have been gillnetted in Canadian waters that weighed in excess of 100 pounds!

Lake trout are not found in streams. Instead they are found in lakes and reservoirs exclusively. Macks prefer cool water temperatures ranging from 40 to 51 degrees. When the surface temperatures of lakes fall within this range, mackinaw can be found in shallow water, but they spend much of the year holding in water that ranges from 100 to 600 feet deep.

Mackinaw display a unique beauty. The flanks range greenish to bluish silver fading to darker along the back and to white on the belly. The flanks and back are liberally marked with bold white or light grey spots. The tail is deeply forked. Macks in the 3 to 10 pound range are common in many western waters. Fish weighing 20 pounds are considered exceptional, while fish of 30 pounds are considered lifetime trophies in most areas.

The mackinaw spawn takes place during the fall when the fish congregate in moderately deep areas of the lake that feature a gravel bottom. Due to the slow growth rate of lakers, individual fish often don't reach spawning maturity until they are 9 or even 10 years old.

Small macks feed on a range of organisms including shrimp, plankton, insects and small crawfish. Mature lakers prefer to dine on baitfish, small trout, kokanee and crawfish.

Mackinaw were originally found in the northern waters of Alaska, Canada and the Great Lakes, but have been widely introduced to deep lakes and reservoirs in the lower 48.

Brook trout are king in terms of popularity on the east coast, but out here in the west they are a little like the odd man out.

Sure they are a lot of fun to catch, but they are most often found in high country lakes and streams where they only attain modest size. Yet for the angler that does some homework there are western lakes where husky brookies can be encountered.

For my money, brookies are among the most beautiful fish that swim. They are characterized by greenish silvery flanks. The color darkens on the back and gradually lightens to creamy white on the belly. Mottled light colored bars extend from the back to the lateral line. Along the sides near the lateral line brookies sport an abundance of black spots along with red spots, trimmed in blue. Like the mackinaw, brook trout are a salmonid, but from a scientific standpoint they aren't considered to be a trout. They are more properly referred to as char just like their big brothers the mackinaw.

Brook trout are late fall and early winter spawners with much of the activity taking place between late October and the end of December. Brookies spawn in streams with the eggs being deposited in areas that have well oxygenated gravel beds. After the eggs are deposited, the female covers them with gravel and as with brown trout they lay dormant until spring.

Originally brook trout were only found on the east coast, but their range has been increased dramatically through stocking programs. Brookies are highly adaptable, provided they have access to cool water year around. They prefer water that falls between 50 and 58 degrees with lots of dissolved oxygen. One of the reasons that brook trout have been able to thrive in the many of the waters where they've been introduced is due to the fact that they are not selective feeders. They will enthusiastically eat aquatic insects, other fish, terrestrial insects, leaches, snails, crawfish and even berries and nuts that find their way into the water.

From the angler's perspective, brookies make up for their diminutive size with their willingness to strike a variety of offerings, their stunning beauty and the outstanding table fare they provide when fried over an open campfire!

So there we have it, a brief overview of the Pacific Coast's dominant trout and char species. Now it is time to learn how to catch them, which is exactly what we'll do in the chapters to come.

Chapter Three: Bank Fishing For Trout

Prospecting the waters of a lake or reservoir for trout from a boat decked out with downriggers and the latest electronics can be both productive and exciting there is no question about that. However, there is something inherently satisfying about successfully targeting trout from the bank.

Bank fishing by its very nature is a more personal approach than trolling. When fishing from the bank it's you against the trout. There's no using a boat to cover a ton of ground or relying on a sonar unit to pinpoint the fish. Bank anglers rely on their legs for mobility and their instincts to locate productive water. When an angler reaches a point where they can consistently score under these circumstances, a feeling of accomplishment is the inevitable result.

Some anglers mistakenly believe that bank fishing is the folly of unfortunate souls that don't have access to a boat and that productive trouting can only be enjoyed while sitting on the water as opposed to sitting next to it. Well, nothing could be further from the truth. I have a beautiful aluminum sled outfitted with all the best toys, yet I routinely spend time fishing from the bank. Sometimes it's nice to just get out and enjoy soaking in the sun while catching a few tasty trout without having to hassle with towing and launching a boat. This is especially true when my schedule only allows me to fish for an hour or two.

As far as the productivity of bank fishing is concerned, rest assured that members of the shore fishing fraternity routinely record catches every bit as impressive as those taken by their boating brethren. In all the years I've been targeting trout, my two largest rainbows came while fishing worms from the bank long before I bought my first boat. The smaller of the two went 7 pounds 12 ounces, while my all-time best 'bow went 8 pounds 15 ounces. Not too bad for a lowly land lover!

All in all banking for trout is a fairly simple endeavor, but like other types of fishing it requires a selection of efficient good quality gear and a solid systematic strategy. The first thing the aspiring bank angler needs is a rod and reel. With dozens of possible combinations available selecting the best outfit for the job at hand can be a daunting task.

Obviously, when bank fishing you'll be doing a lot of casting. This makes spinning tackle the best choice. Since you'll generally be using weights that range from an eighth of an ounce to a half ounce, a light to medium light rod is a good all-around choice.

A lot of folks choose short rods ranging from 5 to 6 feet in length, but I prefer a 7 foot stick. Much of the time you'll be fishing your baits close to the bank, but there are some situations and approaches where casting well offshore gives you a distinct advantage and this is when a longer rod really shines. A 7 foot rod also provides better leverage for fighting fish when you hook into one of the big boys.

While a light rod is required, avoid models with a slow action. Slow action rods are highly flexible throughout their entire length and display a deep parabolic bend when under a load. This type of rod will limit casting distance and reduce hook setting power. A fast action rod that features a flexible tip section followed up with relatively stiff middle and butt sections provides maximum casting distance, solid hook sets and the power required to wear down large trout.

A high level of sensitivity is the final requirement of an efficient bank fishing rod and that means you'll want a rod constructed of graphite. A lot of anglers ask me if expensive, top of the line rods are worth the extra money. The answer is yes and no. You definitely get what you pay for and a high quality rod will catch more fish than a bargain basement model, but you don't have to mortgage the homestead to get a good rod. All major manufacturers such as Fenwick, Shakespeare, Berkeley and Lamiglas to mention only a few, offer high quality graphite spinning rods at prices that won't break your budget.

Once you've settled on a rod, it's time to pick out a reel. As with rods there are a large number of quality spinning reels on the market today. The first requirement is that the reel has a smooth drag. At times 4 pound leader material is required to draw strikes. When fighting good sized trout on line that light you don't want the drag to stick at all when the fish runs. If it does the leader will likely snap. The reel should also have a high gear ratio. The gear ratio refers to the number of times the line is wrapped around the spool for each revolution of the reel handle. At times trout will run straight toward you at the hookset. When that happens a high gear ratio allows you to keep pace with the fish, preventing slack from forming in the line. A 5 to 1 ratio is ideal.

The final consideration in selecting a reel is its line capacity. An average size trout isn't going to pull a lot of line off the reel. So a very small reel with a modest line capacity would do the trick most of the time, but what happens when you hook the trout of a lifetime? When that happens you need plenty of insurance in the form of line capacity. My largest rainbow pulled about 100 yards of 8 pound test line off my reel with its first two runs. If I'd been using an ultra-light reel with a 90 yard capacity that big rainbow would now be known as the big one that got away!

A reel capable of holding at least 200 yards of 6 pound line is a sensible choice that provides plenty of insurance when that big trophy finally comes along.

It's surprising how many anglers will shell out their hard earned cash for a quality rod and reel only to get thrifty when it comes to line. When you consider that the line is the link between you and the fish it just doesn't make sense to go the cheap route. What you are looking for is a quality copolymer monofilament that is fairly limp while offering a high degree of abrasion resistance. Brands of line are a lot like trucks. You know some guys swear by Fords while others love their Chevy's and then there are the Dodge guys. It's the same with line in the sense that once an angler settles on a brand they typically stick with it for a long time. My personal favorites are P-Line CXX and Trilene Maxx. These lines are limp, manageable and exceedingly tough.

Logically it would seem that clear line, being clear, is the best line to choose for maximum stealth, but that's not the case. For most trout fishing situations you'll experience the best result while employing light green line or smoke colored line, because these colors effectively blend into the background colors of the trout's environment.

When the fish are highly pressured or the water is extra clear, fluorocarbon is the way to go since it will give you nearly total invisibility.

Then why not rig up with fluorocarbon all the time? While fluorocarbon gives the advantage of near invisibility it is a lot more expensive than copolymer lines. My policy is to use green tinted line and tip it with a fluorocarbon leader. This gives me total stealth at the lowest possible price point.

Trout trollers are just starting to utilize braided lines. Braid has virtually no stretch, has a superior strength to diameter ratio and us pretty much impervious to the effects of the sun. Braid is more expensive than mono initially, but since braid doesn't break down you'll only have to re-spool every second or third year, saving money in the long run.

Over the past few years I find myself employing braid more and more, but I still don't use it in conjunction with my trout trolling gear, with one exception...My light weight leadcore outfits, but we'll talking more about those in a following chapter.

End tackle represents the nuts and bolts of the bank angler's toolbox. In this chapter we'll focus our discussion on the basics of bait fishing. This approach catches the most trout day in day out all year long from urban reservoirs stocked with rainbows to high mountain lakes teaming with wild brookies.

Since trout spend most of their time holding near the bottom, that's the most effective zone for presenting your bait. The basic bait fishing set up is the sliding sinker rig. To construct sliding sinker rigs that meet a number of different situations and conditions you'll need a selection of hooks, weights, beads and swivels along with a with some fluorocarbon leader material.

I keep my various bait fishing supplies in a plastic compartment box. I like to have both bait holder and octopus hooks on hand in sizes 8, 10 and 12. It is important to use super sharp hooks Gamakatsu hooks are my favorite brand, but they are a little pricy. You can save a little money and use Eagle Claw Lazar Sharp hooks without compromising much in the way of performance.

Egg sinkers are the most popular choice among bait anglers, but I prefer to use the tapered bullet sinkers popular among bass anglers. I find that egg sinkers with their fat round shape tend to hang up in the rocks more than the tapered bullet weight and they also produce more resistance as they move through the water. A selection of sinkers from 1/4 to 1/2 ounce will cover most situations, but I like to add a few in the 1/8 and 3/4 ounce sizes as well.

For a swivel go with a black or anodized model in size No. 1. As for beads, simple plastic ones with an eighth inch diameter work just fine and their color isn't a factor.

I swear by fluorocarbon leader material. Due to its molecular make up fluorocarbon line diffuses light in much the same way as water, making it virtually invisible to fish.

Sometimes, having an invisible leader isn't important, but at other times it is a critical element of success. As a result, I use fluorocarbon leaders at all times. Most often I use 6 pound test, but I also like to have 4 and 8 pound test on hand.

Once you've gathered all the necessary components, putting together a rig is simple. The first step is to pass the line of your spinning rod through one of your sinkers going in from the narrow end and out through the wide end. Next pass your line through a bead and then tie on a swivel using an improved clinch knot. The bead acts as a spacer between the weight and the swivel, protecting the integrity of the knot. To the other end of the swivel attach an 18 to 36 inch section of fluorocarbon leader with an improved clinch knot. The final step is to tie a hook to the end of the leader using a Palomar knot.

There are several popular and productive baits and bait combinations for tempting trout, but the best baits all have one thing in common, they float up off the bottom. Trout will seldom pick a bait directly off the bottom. You want a bait that floats up and away from grass and debris, so that a cruising trout can find it easily.

Worms are low down and dirty. After all, they spend their lives crawling around in dirt or worse...manure. . . Yuck! However worms do have a positive side, namely their value as top notch fishing bait. Bass, trout, panfish, catfish and even bright fresh from the sea steelhead have a soft spot for fat juicy worms.

Traditionally speaking, when it comes to using worms for bait, worms and trout fishing go together like fried chicken and potato salad on the 4th of July! Yet it seems like every year I encounter fewer and fewer trout anglers employing worms. The vast majority of trout targeting boaters I meet troll with lures and plugs exclusively, while most shore anglers I come across spend nearly all of their time soaking floating dough baits.

Has the current generation of trout anglers come to conclusion that their modern sexy offerings outdistance the effectiveness of their grandfathers' night crawlers or have the advertising campaigns of tackle and trout bait companies simply overshadowed the effectiveness of the low crawling worm? I tend to believe that most of the trout anglers entering the sport these days simply overlook worms, because they don't truly grasp how effective they can be. Let's face it you'll never meet a night crawler being represented by an advertising agency!

For the uninitiated anglers out there, I'm going to share a dirty little secret with you. Not only are worms one of the most effective trout baits available, but are also among the simplest to employ effectively.

For the still water bank angler there are really two ways to present a worm, either off the bottom or suspending beneath the water's surface. We'll talk more about suspending worms later on. Most of the time, trout can be found feeding and holding near the bottom, so that's were you should present your bait most of the time.

The key here is presenting your bait NEAR the bottom, not ON the bottom. This is why Fire Bait, PowerBait and other trout dough concoctions float. When teamed with a sliding sinker rig and a 1 to 3 foot leader these baits float up off the bottom right into the cruising zone of the trout.

Taking a cue from your dough soaking brothers, you'll want to float your worm off the bottom too. This can be accomplished by teaming your worm with a marshmallow or injecting your worm with air using a worm blower or hypodermic needle. In most cases I prefer to float my worms with an injection of air, because this makes for a more natural looking offering.

You can buy commercially produced "worm blowers" that are simply a small plastic bottle that has a needle attached. My only complaint about worm blowers is that the needle is usually thick. This punches a big hole in the worm allowing a good portion of the air injected into the worm to escape. A hypodermic needle does a better job, but they are difficult to get. Farm supply stores are the best source for hypodermics that I've found.

I firmly believe that a worm gives me two distinct advantages over dough baits. First of all, experience has demonstrated that worms provide me with the best shot at hooking holdovers and wild trout such as the elusive brown trout that call many of our lakes and reservoirs home simply because worms represent a "natural" bait. A worm is "real" meat and the trout know it.

Secondly unlike dough baits, worms appeal to all of a trout senses. Dough baits put out lots of scent, but their visual attractiveness is limited to an array of bright colors. Worms take things a step farther. Like dough baits worms put off scent, but they also offer eye-catching movement as they wriggle and undulate. These subtle movements can be the difference between a hookup and a rejection, especially when the trout concerned in an experienced holdover or wild fish.

At times when the water is stained or even when it isn't, adding scent to the worms greatly aids trout in finding them and results in more strikes. You can certainly apply paste scents to the outside of the worm with good results, but a trick I like to employ is injecting my worms with bait oil. Oil is lighter than water and will actually float the worm off the bottom. As it slowly leaks out of the worm a scent trail is formed that leads cruising trout back to the bait. Anise oil is my favorite scent for this technique. It's a sweet scent and I've found that all species of fish including trout respond well to it.

Three decades ago, worms, salmon eggs and soft cheese were the kings as far as trout baits were concerned, and then it happened. Floating dough baits arrived on the scene and things haven't been the same since. PowerBait is the most popular and certainly one of the most effective of these putty like concoctions.

When PowerBait first came out my buddy Red and I each picked up a bottle of orange dough. We didn't give the bait a try for quite a while. Finally we were fishing at an urban lake on one of those days when nothing seemed to be working. I put a small ball of the bait on a slip sinker rig and pitched it out not expecting to get a bite. Well, the rig didn't even have a chance to hit the bottom, before a feisty rainbow grabbed the dough and took off. Over the next two hours Red and I had a fantastic time, catching and releasing 27 trout. From that day forward, I've never doubted the effectiveness of Power Bait. It is something that should be in every bait angler's bag of tricks.

In the wake of PowerBait's success a number of different dough baits have hit the market over the years. I've tried most of them without much success, but that all changed recently when I tried a new bait from the Pautzke Bait Company called Fire Bait.

Having encountered so many new floating dough baits that just don't make the grade I'd begun to doubt whether any new dough bait would be useful. Honestly I did my best to hold onto this attitude when I heard about Fire Bait, but the fact that the Pautzke Company put their name on the product meant a lot. Pautzke salmon eggs have been the industry standard since 1934. In recent years the folks at Pautzke have worked to expand their line up with products like Kokanee Fuel scent, Fire Cure egg cure and Fire Corn kokanee corn. All of these products have proven to be top notch performers, so why not at least give Fire Bait a try?

The next thing I knew I was firing emails back and forth to the folks at Pautzke headquarters up in Ellensburg, Washington and a box of sample bait was on its way to my office. I was pretty excited as I waited for my box of bait to arrive. The trout fishing has been exceptionally good all around the north state and when the Fire Bait arrived it would give me an excuse to get out of the office and onto the water. That's always a good thing!

When the box arrived and I busted it open and found 14 distinctly different types of Fire Bait including Red, Pink, Orange, Natural, Chartreuse Garlic, Rainbow, Peach Garlic, Yellow, Green, American Wildfire, Garlic Wildfire, Mountain Wildfire, Atomic Garlic and Mallow Balls O' Fire. These colors are enhanced with a sprinkling of glitter.

The first thing that struck me about the new bait was its color range. The colors were bright and vibrant. Screwing the caps off a few jars I felt the bait and rolled some of it into a ball. I found the bait to be soft and tacky. Forming it into a smooth tight ball was no problem.

Color is one factor in a dough bait's effectiveness across a range of water conditions, but I believe that the scent a bait puts off is THE most important factor.

Over the years the folks at Pautzke have gone to great lengths to perfect krill scents and krill is front and center in Fire Bait's scent profile. Krill are of course tiny shrimp. In areas of the ocean where it is found, krill is always one of the major foundational building blocks of the food chain.

In freshwater trout feed heavily on scud (there are more than 800 different types of these freshwater shrimp) as well as plankton. It could be said that trout, particularly rainbow trout, are hardwired to feed on shrimp.

Beyond the scent of krill, Fire Bait is fortified with genuine Balls O Fire salmon egg juice. When the krill and Balls O Fire scents are combined it not only makes for a scent that pushed all of a trout's feeding buttons, but it is also a scent combination that can't be duplicated by anyone else in the industry.

For day in day out fishing the krill/egg scented Fire Bait should serve you well. For times when the water is off color and you need a bolder scent, garlic has been integrated into four colors of Fire Bait. Trout anglers have long used garlic scent. I remember back in the old days when I'd mix garlic oil into my Velveeta cheese to make it more effective.

Scent only works if it is dispersed into the water column. Fire Bait, being 90% biodegradable constantly releases both scent and glitter into the water. This creates scent trail with a bit of flash. When trout cut that scent trail they follow it right back to your bait.

When I received my first samples of Fire Bait I concluded that the bait looked good and smelled good, but the only way to determine if it would actually be effective was to take it out to a lake and test it under field conditions against other popular baits head to head.

Tom a fellow writer and trout fishing nut joined me to test the bait on a late January day at Rollins Lake in the Sierra foothills. Rollins had been planted heavily and it seem to be an ideal place for testing.

Utilizing our two rod stickers we fished Fire Bait, inflated worms, other dough baits and salmon eggs. Early on we got a few nibbles, but the water was cold and the trout seemed lethargic.

I noticed right away that Fire Bait is super buoyant and as impressive as the colors are in the bottle they seemed even more vibrant in the water

Once the sun hit the water things started to warm up a bit and the trout bite came on strong. We got one hit on a worm and a few bites on other types of dough bait, but the vast majority of the action we experienced came on Fire Bait. We employed Orange, Chartreuse Garlic, Yellow and Rainbow and they all got hit, but Orange and Yellow proved to be the best colors that day.

By the end of the day Tom and I had landed 12 trout and had kept full limits of fish in the 11 to 14 inch range. Overall we probably had between 25 and 30 individual bites.

As I mentioned over time I've tried a bunch of different dough baits that promised to be the "next big thing in trout fishing". Most of them have been of questionable quality and predictably they've failed miserably.

Fire Bait on the other hand is a high quality bait that definitely catches fish. I haven't tossed anything out of my bait fishing line up and replaced it with Fire Bait. What I've done and what I recommend that you do is to integrate Fire Bait into the lineup of baits that you currently carry, because experience says there are days when the trout prefer Fire Bait to everything else.

Both PowerBait and Fire Bait come in a long list of colors and combination colors. Most dough baiters have handful of colors that they have a lot of confidence in and as a result they use these personal favorites almost exclusively. Rainbow is very popular as is chartreuse. My strategy is to keep things simple. I like to have chartreuse and orange colors on hand for stained water and subtler yellows and pinks when the water is clear. The nice thing about dough bait is that it's relatively cheap so you can afford to carry solid selection of colors.

These days salmon eggs are a largely over looked bait among the lake fishing crowd, due in large part to the popularity of dough baits. There is no doubt about it, trout love salmon eggs, but they have one drawback. They don't float and you can't inject them with air. As a result it is standard practice to combine a salmon egg or two with a scented marshmallow. Marshmallows are buoyant and provide floatation for the salmon egg. Back in the days before dough baits, salmon egg and marshmallow combinations were so popular in northern California that anglers began calling them a "Shasta Fly".

Since this is the introductory chapter on bank fishing, I'll suffice to say that your arsenal should boast red, orange and yellow salmon eggs. In following chapters we'll take in depth looks at both salmon egg and roe fishing techniques. Rest assured while salmon eggs might be a bit out of vogue for trout anglers, the trout still love them!

Whether or not you fish with salmon eggs, every serious bait angler should carry a small selection of scented marshmallows. They will take trout when used alone or they can be effectively combined with other baits. On several occasions when my standard offerings weren't working, combining night crawlers or Power Bait with cheese or garlic scented marshmallows has saved the day. I can't understand why marshmallows are so effective in some situations, but I don't spend a lot of time thinking about it. I just make sure I have some of them squirreled away with my bait fishing gear.

Now that we've taken a look at rods, reels, rigs and baits it's time to get out to the lake and put these tools to work. One of the big reasons that the casual bank angler doesn't catch trout consistently is the fact that they don't put much thought into the areas they choose to fish. They get to the lake, scan all the available terrain, feel overwhelmed and pick a spot at random. Sometimes there are trout holding at the spot they pick and they catch a few fish. More often than not the spot they settle on is devoid of fish and they are forced to find solace in the saying that goes, "the worst day fishing is better than the best day working"...That's fine for them, but we want to catch trout!

The most successful bank anglers are the ones that take a systematic approach to selecting fishing spots. Since there is only a limited amount of ground that a bank angler can cover it makes sense to focus on plying high percentage areas. The most productive bank fishing spots are generally located near transition zones that feature an abrupt depth change, in areas where the lake narrows or where small tributaries flow into the lake.

Over the years I've had some of my best bank action while working areas where a shallow flat drops into deep water. During low light periods trout typically move onto flats to feed. When the sun is on the water they tend to retreat to holding areas adjacent to the security of deep water. Spots where flats transition into deep water are high percentage areas because they provide the trout with immediate access to both shallow water feeding habitat and the safety of the depths.

Narrows or bottlenecks, while not occurring at all lakes, typically feature hot action wherever they are found. The reason productive action generally can be found in bottlenecks is simple. These areas concentrate the trout and whenever you can find a large number of trout passing through a limited area, your chance of success rises significantly.

The best bottlenecks feature an abrupt and extreme narrowing of the lake. Ideally you are looking for a lake with an hourglass shape where two large basins are connected by a relatively narrow band of water. Another classic bottleneck is often found in small to medium size impoundments where the river arm that feeds the reservoir meets the main body. In this situation the angler wants to be positioned right at the mouth of the river arm.

Areas where small tributaries enter a lake are attractive to trout for a number of reasons and should always be explored. Inflowing tributaries introduce both food in the form of small fish, invertebrates and terrestrial insects as well as oxygenated water into the lake. As a result trout tend to stack up around tributaries.

When it storms during the dead of winter, seasonal inflowing tributaries often flush water into lakes that is substantially warmer than the lake itself. As a result trout flock to these areas to enjoy the relative warmth and the warmth tends to spark their appetites. This sort of thing happens at most lakes. Personally I've experienced great action working areas that feature inflowing run off at both Lake Shasta in Northern California and Bullards Bar Reservoir to the south.

During the early spring big rainbows move toward tributaries to spawn while brown trout do the same thing during the late fall. These are prime times for the bank angler to pick up trophy quality fish they might not have access to during the rest of the year.

Finally, tributaries that enter reservoirs whether they are actively flowing or not mark the location of submerged creek beds that eventually meet the submerged river channel of the lake's primary tributary. These submerged creek beds typically feature deeper water than the surrounding area and act as major travel corridors for trout and other gamefish. Areas within submerged creeks that play host to rock piles, stumps or fallen trees are particularly attractive to brown trout and are well worth seeking out.

Narrows and tributaries are obviously easy to identify features. Areas where shallow water transitions into deeper water often are not readily apparent to the casual observer. Without the aid of a sonar unit you'll have to rely on your eye and instinct to pinpoint these potential hotspots. Just as a golfer reads subtleties of the course, the bank angler reads terrain along the shoreline in order to predict how the lake bottom looks below the waterline. Steep hillsides that proceed into the lake likely continue downward below the water at roughly the same angle and the same is true for gently sloping banks. At times the fall of the terrain will fool you by changing abruptly under the water, but most of the time your deductions will be correct.

Once you've identified some promising areas to explore, it's time to bait a hook and get down to business. Early and late in the day or during periods of overcast weather it is smart to make your first casts into relatively shallow water, before moving deeper. When the sun is on the water it is wise to start out plying moderately deep water. Of course the water temperature plays a critical role in how deep you should position your offering.

As we learned earlier, most trout prefer a water temperature of around 56 degrees. If the surface temperature is in the 50's you can be certain that trout will be holding in the top 20 feet of the water column, so you'll want your bait resting in water that is 20 feet deep or less. If the surface temperature is in the 60's or lower 70's you can bet the bank that the majority of the trout will be holding in deeper cooler water most of the time and baits should be positioned accordingly.

Many bank anglers seem to have an obsession with flinging their baits as far from shore as possible. At times this is a good strategy, but when the water is cool these anglers often cast their bait out into deep water well past the depth zone where most of the trout are holding, so once again before you make your presentation consider the conditions and let them be your guide.

When it comes to the type of bait I use I'm always ready to experiment, but there are some general guidelines that will help you get off on the right track. In lakes primarily inhabited by wild browns, brookies or holdover rainbows worms are the top choice. While these trout may not encounter worms very often they are still a natural bait that the trout recognize.

In situations where most of the trout have been recently planted, floating dough baits are a solid choice, although worms will work too. I rig up with an octopus hook when dough baits or salmon eggs are on the menu. When the main course consists of worms I like to run with a bait holder style hook.

Sometimes whole worms work well and at other times a half night crawler or mini crawlers works best. I like to start off using a 1. 5 inch piece of worm and given a choice when I cut worms in half I only like to use the head (pointed) end of the worm because that half is more muscular and tends to hold air better and stay on the hook better.

When hooking a worm don't gob it on the hook, stitching it on with multiple punctures. Instead lightly pin it, passing the hook through the middle section of the bait one time. Once the worm is on the hook, it's time to inject it with air.

When baiting up with dough bait, form a quarter inch ball of bait and simply shove your octopus hook into the center of the ball. Finish up by squeezing the dough in tight around the eye of the hook to hold the bait in place.

Once you've baited your hook and lobbed your rig into the water, you'll want to place your rod in a holder, while waiting for a bite. A forked stick stuck into the bank will suffice, but I prefer to bring along a compact metal holder as it saves me a lot of time hunting around on the bank for sticks.

A common mistake is fishing with a tight line. This works great for catfish and other less sensitive fish, but when a trout feels any kind of resistance it will likely as not spit out the bait. To prevent spooking trout it is important to have some slack in the line so any trout that picks up the bait can move off and swallow the bait without feeling anything.

One trick to accomplishing this is to hang a small plastic bobber on the line between the tip of the rod and the second or third eye. Enough slack is pulled off the reel to allow the bobber to hang down almost to the ground. When a trout takes the bait and moves off the slack is paid out gradually as the bobber pulls upward toward the rod. When the line comes tight it's time to set the hook and begin fighting your prize.

For an even stealthier approach, when the trout are particularly skittish or sluggish due to cold water you can dispense with the bobber and fish your bait with an open bail. When using this method place your rod in the holder, open the reel, pull off enough slack for the line to reach the ground and then place a small twig or stone on it. This way your line will be prevented from flowing wildly off the reel in the breeze, but when a fish takes the bait it can swim off with zero resistance.

A final point to remember is that the most successful bank anglers tend to stay on the move. You don't want to pick out a spot and spend the entire day fishing it if the trout are not responding. Instead you should give a spot anywhere from 30 minutes to an hour to produce. If nothing happens it's time to move on in search of greener pastures.

Chapter Four: Advanced Banking

Up to this point our exploration of bank fishing has more or less centered around tossing out a piece of bait and waiting for a hungry trout to come along to gulp it down. While this strategy produces tens of thousands of trout for west coast anglers every year, it is only the tip of the iceberg.

Once you've accumulated some tackle and some experience locating trout, it's time to take things to a higher level. While trout do a lot of their foraging near the bottom there are times when they move up in the water column to feed. One of the most effective tools anglers can add to their arsenals to deal with these situations is the slip bobber.

Slip bobbers have been popular in Europe for decades, but anglers in the United States are just discovering how effective they can be. As its name implies a slip bobber has the ability to move up and down the line and therein lies a large measure of the bobber's effectiveness.

The system works like this, the spinning rod's line is passed through a small plastic sleeve that has a pre-tied string knot attached to it, known as a bobber stop. Once on the line the string knot is slid off the plastic tube and snugged down tight on the monofilament. The plastic tube is slid back off the line and discarded. Next a bead is slid onto the monofilament followed by a slip bobber. After that a swivel is tied to the end of the main line and one or more split shot are place an inch or two above it. Finally an 18 inch 4 to 6 pound fluorocarbon leader tipped with a hook is tied to the swivel.

Once you're finished what you end up with is a rig that has the ability to fish a bait at virtually any depth without compromising casting distance. For example, let's say you are fishing on a bank that drops off into deep water. Since the water temperature is in the low 50's you suspect that the trout are cruising 15 feet deep over 35 feet of water about 50 feet offshore.

Using a standard sliding sinker rig these fish would be difficult if not impossible to catch, but with the slip bobber rig you simply slide the bobber stop up the line to a point 15 feet above the hook. Since bobber stop is made out of string, it is soft and you can reel it right onto the spool of your reel and cast without it hanging up on the eyes of the rod. After reeling the bobber up to within a few inches of the rod tip, bait the hook and cast the rig out to the area where the trout are. When the rig hits the water the split shot will take the bait down, pulling line through the bobber. Once the bait reaches the desired depth the bobber stop and bead wedge against the top of the bobber and the bait is left suspended 15 feet below the surface right in the suspected strike zone of the trout.

Most baits such as night crawlers, meal worms, salmon eggs and even crickets work well when used with slip bobbers. On the other hand buoyant baits such as dough bait and marshmallows should be avoided. When these baits float upward they inevitably wrap around the main line and create tangles.

In lakes and reservoirs where it is legal to use them 1 to 3 inch minnows are absolutely deadly. A frisky minnow will draw strikes from all species and sizes of trout from 10 inch planter rainbows to massive hook jawed browns.

I like to go with an octopus hook when using minnows because they have a wider bite than bait holders that result in a higher percentage of hooked trout. There are a couple of different ways to hook minnows. The classic rigging calls for them to be pinned lightly through the back near the dorsal fin. The alternate method is to hook them through the lips upward from bottom to top.

I've found that lip hooked minnows not only live longer and swim more vigorously, but they also result in more hookups. When compared to other minnow eaters like bass and crappie, trout have relatively small mouths. Unlike bass that inhale a minnow, trout typically grab a minnow and then turn it in preparation for swallowing it head first. Lip hooking minnows ensures that the trout will have the hook well inside its mouth when the hook is set.

You can't rush the hook set when using minnows. If the water is in the middle 50's the trout will typically grab the minnow and make a hard run. When this happens you'll want to feed the trout line for about a 15 count before making your move, to allow the trout to get the minnow turned. When he water dips into the 40's the trout typically won't run vigorously. Instead, your bobber will slowly pull beneath the surface. Many times it will only descend a few inches and then stop. You've got to resist the temptation to set the hook or tighten the line. When the trout are sluggish due to cold water you might have to let them mouth the minnow for a minute or more to ensure they get the bait turned and well back in their mouth.

The primary forage for trout in many of the west coast's lakes and reservoirs are open water baitfish in the form of threadfin shad and Japanese pond smelt. When trout are actively feeding and chasing bait, very good results can be achieved while fishing lures. While lures can catch some trout at any time of the day and under almost any conditions, the best action typically occurs during low light periods such as early and late in the day or when the sky is overcast. One of the big cues to tie on a lure is when trout can be seen jumping, splashing and pursuing minnows.

The best lures for shore anglers that want to imitate minnows are without a doubt wobbling spoons. There are a ton of different spoons on the market, unfortunately for the bank fishing enthusiast many of them were designed exclusively for trolling and are too light for casting. In an emergency these light spoons can be used with split shot clamped on the line for extra weight, but this is a makeshift solution. It is much better to lay in a small supply of heavier spoons that cast well.

My all-time favorite casting spoons are Cripplures and Kastmasters. The Cripplure has a unique side to side rolling action that virtually screams injured baitfish. The Kastmaster flies through the air like a bullet, hence the name. When the Kastmaster hits the water it has a traditional side to side kicking action. The Cripplure only comes in one size. The Kastmaster comes in a wide range of sizes I've found the 1/8 and 1/4 ounce model to be the most effective, but I usually have a few 1/2 ouncers kicking around too.

As good as Kastmasters and Cripplures are there some other spoons you might want to consider adding to your selection. Luhr Jensen Krocodile Spoons are well known trout killers. Crocodiles are made from solid stamped brass. They are fairly thick and as a result are heavy for their size. Translation? They cast like an artillery shell!

For general purpose trout plugging, I like the 3/8 and ½ ounce models, but if you are plying water that has a reputation for producing big fish don't hesitate to toss a ¾ or 1 ounce model.

Moving on, I've had a good deal of success tossing large ½ ounce Hum Dingers from shore. These lures perform best with a fairly brisk retrieve, so for Hum Dingers to be effective the trout have to be in an active mode.

If the trout seem to be a bit lethargic and slow to react Little Cleo Spoons are a great choice. They have a large profile humpback design that gives them a very seductive wiggling action at slow speeds.

For the beginner I'd suggest getting a few of the spoons I've mentioned and then start using them. Over time you'll establish your favorite lures and lure sizes.

Don't make the assumption that my list of spoons for bank fishing is comprehensive. It's not. Almost any appropriately sized spoon will catch trout at times. If you see something that catches your eye, buy it and see if the trout like it. The spoons that I've mentioned are the ones that I rely on and are pretty much industry standards, meaning that you won't have any problem finding them.

Fishing spoons is pretty straight forward, but there are some special kinks that can be incorporated into your repertoire that will result in a few bonus trout every year. The first thing to think about is your lure to line connection. Kastmasters come with a split ring attached and Krocodiles have a swivel attached to them out of the package. The other spoons I mentioned simply have a hole in them. If you tie a tight knot directly to that hole, it will kill a lot of the lure's action. You'll still catch fish, but if you employ a connection that allows the lure a free range of movement you'll catch more.

You can tie on your spoons via a loop knot. I've done it and at times continue to do it, but tying the knot is a pain. It's a skill I think you should have in reserve for emergencies, but overall you'll be best served by picking up a small selection of high quality light wire lock snaps. Lock snaps, not snap swivels...While I don't think the appearance of a snap scares the trout, I still don't like to add to the snap's profile by adding a swivel.

 Trollers score with spoons and other lures by covering as much ground as they can. The shore caster also needs to cover as much water as possible, but with a very different philosophy. When trollers talk about covering water they are usually referring to distance. For the bank plugger covering water mean covering the available water thoroughly.

The first rule of plugging from the bank is to fan cast. This means that you don't want to stand on the bank casting methodically to the same spot. Facing the lake you have access to a 180 degree arch of water and you should cover it methodically. Begin by making a cast nearly parallel to the shoreline to the right or left. Make the next cast a yard or two farther out into the lake and proceed until you've covered the entire arch. On the first time around the arch begin retrieving a second or two after the spoon hits the water. The next time around count the spoon down before starting the retrieve. Using this method both near shore and offshore water will be covered and a range of depths will be explored as well.

In terms of retrieve speed, it is usually best to start out working fairly briskly. If a fast retrieve isn't working, gradually slow down until you find a speed the trout respond to. Working spoons with a steady retrieve will catch fish, but speeding up, slowing down and adding the occasional twitch will give the impression of an injured baitfish, drawing more strikes.

What color lures to use is often a point of much confusion and second guessing for anglers. Once again my approach is systematic. I begin with natural colors that match the shad and smelt the trout feed on. If those colors fail to produce I start experimenting with bright offerings. Chrome, chrome and blue, gold, brass, brass and red, brass and orange and firetiger have been the most consistent spoon colors for me over the years.

Black and dark colored spoons definitely should have a place in your tackle box. During the low light periods of dawn and dusk and during overcast days trout like to zero in on the dark silhouette of black, dark green and frog pattern spoons.

I do a large percentage of my plugging with spoons, but spinners can be effective too. Spinners don't really mimic baitfish the way spoons do, but they put out a lot of vibration and this accounts for a good deal of their effectiveness. There are a number of different spinners on the market that have well-earned reputations for tempting trout including Panther Martins, Roostertails, Mepps and Blue Foxes.

As with spoons you'll want a selection of 1/8 and 1/4 ounce models. I don't believe that color is as critical with spinners as it is with spoons, but I still adhere to the natural colors, followed by bright colors strategy. The casting pattern and varied retrieve that is used with spoons should be employed while fishing spinners too.

Spoons and spinners will tempt trout of all sizes, but if you are in the market for a true heavyweight be it a big brown or a trophy rainbow, minnow plugs will put you on the road to Monsterville. Minnow plugs come in a big selection of sizes from tiny 1 inchers to really large models that are 6 to 7 inches in length. The really small ones do a good job imitating small baitfish. However, they tend to be light and don't cast very well. In general, if your goal is to imitate small baitfish, you're better off using spoons.

To get the most out of minnow plugs you want a selection of 3 and 4 inch baits. Big trout, say those 4 pounds and larger certainly eat a lot of minnows, yet if a plump trout, squawfish or chub shows up when a trophy trout is in a feeding mood it will seldom pass up a big meal.

For years Rapala minnow plugs were synonymous with big trout. Rapalas remain a top producer, but these days there are other manufacturers vying for the attention of both trout and the anglers that pursue them. In reality some of the best new baits are suspending rip baits designed for bass fishing. It didn't take bass anglers long to discover that these baits are not only deadly on bass, but they catch their share of hefty trout too.

I'll never forget the first rainbow I caught on a bass size minnow plug. I was working a rocky bank at Lake Berryessa hoping for a husky smallmouth, when it happened...Twitch, twitch, pause, twitch...WHAM! Bass on!

"Wait a second that bass is fighting funny. I think it might be a trout. "

It was, and after craning the square tailed rainbow into the boat, my tape measure revealed that it was just short of 22 inches long! It was way bigger than any of the trout I'd caught in the lake while trolling. Naturally, I've been sold on the deadliness of bass style minnow plugs for trout fishing ever since.

The well-heeled minnow plug aficionado's lure selection will include some Rapala floaters in sizes No. F5, F7 and F9 along with some Rapala Husky Jerks in sizes No. HJ6 or HJ8. From the Yo-Zuri line of baits the Pin Minnow in the No. F196 size and the Hardcore Jerkbait in the F684 size. If money isn't a problem the Lucky Craft Company produces some fine baits for the trout angler, namely the Pointer in size No. PT65 and the Deep Pointer in size No. 65DD.

The array of colors in your minnow plug selection need not be extensive, but you do need both natural and bright colored offerings. Rainbow trout, silver body black back and gold body black back are pretty standard on the subdued side. On the bright end of the spectrum firetiger and clown are great choices. These bright patterns don't resemble anything in nature, but there is something about them that triggers strikes.

The bright orange Rapala is surrounded with a special mythology and for good reason...they have a track record of producing huge browns and rainbows that should be smart enough to never grab such a bright gaudy offering, but grab it they do.

Over my years as editor of the Fish Sniffer magazine I've received dozens of photos of trophy caliber trout that have been caught on 2 to 4 inch florescent orange Rapala floaters. Some of these fish have come out of stained water, but most of them were caught in crystal clear lakes and reservoirs.

Why the trout fall for such a loud colored lure is anyone's guess? The important thing is to squirrel a few away in your trout gear and cast them with confidence!

The rainbow trout pattern is my number one choice and I have a lot of confidence in it. Confidence is a very important factor in the model and color of minnow plug you choose to throw. While minnow plugs do draw big strikes, there is often an extended period of time between trout. If you don't have confidence in your bait, it is tough to keep working it cast after cast as you wait for that all too infrequent strike.

Minnow plugs can be effectively worked with a number of different retrieves, but I've had my best luck by burning them, popping them and stopping them. The cadence goes something like this. I cast out the bait and crank it down hard until it reaches its maximum depth. Then I give it a couple of sharp twitches before letting it come to a complete stop. After the pause I might twitch it a time or two before I begin cranking or I might just start cranking it.

Strikes can come at any time, but I've hooked most of my fish when the plug begins to move after a pause. One of the reasons that Lucky Crafts are so effective and pricy is the fact that they will stop absolutely dead in the water for extended periods of time while neither rising nor falling. Lucky Crafts really shine when the water is in the lower 40's because of their ability to suspend. When the water is really cold, the longer you can pause the plug the more effective your presentation is and Lucky Craft lures are really conducive to this type of retrieve.

Big trout move into shallow shoreline areas when the light level is low and the odds of ambushing a meal are in their favor. Late evening and early morning are great times to intercept them. Some of the best opportunities occur during stormy weather. Grey skies spitting rain or snow, gusty winds and white caps elevate the heart rate of dedicated trophy hunters, because at times like these they know that the largest trout in the lake will likely be cruising shoreline structure looking to pounce on an easy meal.

Plugging and hiking go hand in hand. It's hard to beat plugging if you are an angler that has a sense of adventure and likes to get in a little exercise. While plugging, it is possible to cover water relatively quickly and your effective range is only limited by how far your legs will take you. Many times I've covered several miles while hiking and plugging. This is a great way to learn a new lake. While hiking, you'll often stumble on lightly fished areas that produce trout year after year on both lures and bait.

Once you get a quarter mile from a parking area you are out of the range of the vast majority of shore anglers and most boat anglers like to stay a fair piece offshore, not wanting to loose lures or downrigger balls on the bottom. As a result there are a lot of lightly fished areas just waiting to be uncovered by the ambitious bank plugger.

Chapter Five: Alternative Trout Baits...

Bait fishing for trout...it's often as effective as it is simple. Arm a hook with an inflated worm or a ball of dough and toss it into a likely spot. Many times that's all it takes to catch trout while fishing from the bank.

It's probably this "first glance simplicity" that promotes the idea that somehow those "dough slingers and worm drowners" just don't have as much skill or finesse as trollers, fly flingers and lure tossers.

I use all these approaches for trout, so there is no way that I'm going to debate, which requires the most skill or savvy. Myself and a legion of other trouters out there feel that the best method for catching trout is the one that is working right now and like it or not, soaking bait ALMOST ALWAYS WORKS...Day in, day out all year long, rain or shine, whether the water is crystal clear or stained and muddy...

Bank or boat fishing with the old standbys like dough, salmon eggs and worms is indeed simple yet there are a number of variations you can employ that will make your bait fishing expeditions even more fun and productive.

Before I hit you with bait and presentation options, allow me to share my thoughts and observations about these standby baits and why they work. Let's start with salmon eggs. Salmonoids...trout, salmon and steelhead are all hardwire on an instinctive level to eat eggs. It doesn't matter if it's a 50 pound king in the Sacramento River or a 9 inch planter rainbow at Lake Chabot that has never seen an egg before. Both of these fish will gobble cured salmon eggs with gusto.

Scent is probably the most driving factor that prompts trout to grab an egg, but shape and color can be important secondary factors.

Dough baits operate a lot like salmon eggs, with scent being the primary factor in creating strikes, but again shape, size and color also need to be considered.

The folks at Berkley that make PowerBait aren't talking about what scent it is that PowerBait exudes beyond saying that it was created in Berkley's "labs".

PowerBait came on so strong and is so effective that Dan Bacher and I contend that it was likely something found at the flying saucer crash site in Roswell that Dr. Keith Jones and Berkley's lab boys reverse engineered. Until the folks at Berkley come forward to dispute this claim, Dan and I are sticking with our theory.

Enough about Berkley's "Rainbow Roswell Dough"...What about Pautzke's Fire Bait. There's no secret why it is so effective. Casey Kelley, the captain at Team Pautzke will tell you without hesitation that it attracts trout with a potent combination of salmon egg juice and krill.

Egg scent and krill are very provocative scents to trout. Combine the scent attraction with the array of vibrant colors that Fire Bait is offered in and you've got a winning combination.

And this brings us to the worm. I love them and so do trout. You can float them off the bottom by injecting them with air. If you want to add scent you can inflate them with a combination of air and bait oil. I like worms because they offer both scent and movement. As that worm floats in the water column it constantly moves and wriggles. Trout have a keen eye for movement and if the water is clear they can see that worm from long range.

When I first started experimenting with trout baits more than 20 years ago, I played around with combinations of the basic baits. For example one afternoon at Collins Lake my wife Gena and I were fishing in Elmer's Cove. The action was slow and I encouraged her to try something new. She came up with a bait she called a "Cherry Bomb". It was simply a ¼ inch ball of yellow PowerBait with a single red Pautzke salmon egg pinned on the hook point.

The trout went on a Cherry Bomb binge and Gena kicked my butt. I was stubborn and stayed with PowerBait a la carte, when it was the combination that the rainbows wanted.

The Cherry Bomb remains Gena's favorite combination to this day! I make a similar bait teaming either PowerBait or Fire Bait with a single kernel of corn. You can use the same shoe peg corn that kokanee trollers use or better yet, pick up a bottle of Pautzke's kokanee corn. It comes in different colors and is impregnated with krill.

Recently the "Power Mouse" burst onto the scene. This combination of a ball of PowerBait or a Power Egg with a Berkley Trout Worm came out of southern California and proved to be so popular that Berkley has started selling ready-made Power Mice that feature Power Eggs fused with a worm tail.

My fishing buddies and I have been using this type of bait for at least 10 years we just didn't talk about it. My favorite is a

"Meal Mouse" to make one you team a ball of PowerBait or Fire Bait with a meal worm. The bait floats the worm and the worm gives the bait movement as well as a unique shape.

You can further play with the bait by forming the dough into different shapes. You can also swap out the meal worm for a red worm, a Trout Worm, a piece of night crawler or even a thin ribbon of anchovy fillet.

Don't tell anybody, but you can use the combination of white dough bait and an anchovy fillet to catch the occasional king at Folsom Lake early in the year when the water is cold enough for the kings to come near the bank.

My dad was aware of my dough bait experiments, so when he first moved to the foothills he did some experimenting of his own and came up with a couple deadly combinations.

The first one he showed me I call the glitter bomb. I'd noticed a "shaker" full of multicolored glitter in his tackle box. When I asked him about it he showed me the bait.

After digging a clump of PowerBait out of a jar he smeared the bait on his palm. He then dribbled a bit of anise scent on it and liberally shook glitter over it, before rolling it into a ball. It looks like it sounds...A ball of dough bait that has a ton of flash and sparkle. Better still as the bait dissolves the glitter is released to drift with the scent trail. This sounds like a little thing, but all you're trying to do it get the attention of the trout.

Dad developed the second bait while fishing an Auburn area pond that had some current in it. He wanted a dough bait that would offer some movement and he thought marabou seemed like just the thing. He thought about tying some marabou on a standard hook. That way he could place a dough ball above or below it and the end result would be a dough bait with a marabou tail that would come alive in the water.

Finally he decided that tying the marabou on the hook was tedious and time consuming, so he grabbed a small black woolly bugger streamer fly out of his fly fishing gear. He formed a ball of dough around the middle of the fly allowing plenty of hackle to protrude both above and below the dough and of course the marabou tail had unrestricted movement. The "Dough Fly" caught trout then and it catches them now and you don't need to fish it near current.

All of the bait variations I've discussed are effective and if your standard baits aren't working I would encourage you to experiment with them or combinations of your own. Your imagination is the only limiting factor!

I'll leave you with a final tip. Most folks think of bait fishing as a static affair where you cast out and wait for a bite. That's how we do it most of the time, but there is no reason that you can't add a little movement to your presentation.

If the wait'em out approach just isn't working as well as it should, try casting out and then inching the bait back in. You can try slow and steady or hop it up off the bottom, let it set for a minute or two and repeat until you've retrieved the bait.

Combining dough baits or inflated worms with a retrieve of some sort has produced so many trout for me that I never just reel in to check my bait. I'll give the rig a few hops and stops before bringing it in, just to cover all my bases. The result is a few extra trout throughout the season!

Chapter Six: The 'Ol Clear Bubble Trick

I'd like to shake the guy's hand that invented modern spinning tackle and maybe treat him to an In-N-Out Burger. I don't go around buying folks In-N-Out Burgers as a general practice, so this shows you how much I appreciate a good spinning rig. The modern spinning setup is light, strong, simple to use for novices and experts alike and reliability approaches 100%.

If spinning gear, or any type of conventional gear has an inherent weakness it's the inability to toss really small lightweight trout baits. I'm talking about things like bits of night crawler, mealworms, flies and the tiniest of spoons like Dick Nites and Vance's Sockeye Slammers. These offerings are simply too light to cast for any distance. And at first glance that precludes you from casting such offerings especially if you are bank fishing. But alas where there's a will there's specialized tackle for us anglers to buy!

One solution is to team those light offerings with some weight in the form of split shot to allow for comfortable long range casting. The problem with this approach is that to present an offering anywhere near the surface you have to retrieve line quickly before the bait, fly or lure sinks off the map. Unfortunately when using the small stuff, fast retrieves generally aren't what you want.

The best solution to the problem comes in the form of a clear plastic bobber or "casting bubble" as they've been dubbed by some. I call the approach the 'ol clear bubble trick. The clear bubbles that I'm referring to are oval in shape. The bubble has a hole at either end and a tapered hollow spike wedges into those holes. Your main line can be threaded through the spike.

Basic bubble rigging goes like this. Take your bubble and pull the spike out exposing the holes. Submerge the bobber in water and shake it around to force out the air and let in water. The holes are small and it can be tough to get the water to flow in so you'll have to work at it a little. I like to fill my bobbers completely, but we'll talk more about that in a bit.

Without removing the bobber from the water, shove the hollow spike through the holes until it is firmly wedged, trapping the water inside. It's this trapped water that is going to add casting weight to your rig.

Next thread your main line through the hollow spike impaled in the bubble. After passing the line though the spike thread on a plastic bead and then knot on a small black swivel. Your leader will attach the other end of the swivel.... We'll get back to the leader soon.

When you thread the bobber on your line you want the WIDE end of the spike resting against the bead. That way when you cast it the pressure tightens the spike, rather than forcing it out and letting your water escape.

Eagle Claw offers clear bubbles in 1, 2 and 2. 5 inch sizes. I go with the 1 inchers and I fill my bubble up completely about 95% of the time. A 1 inch bubble filled with water weighs quite a bit. I haven't weighed one but I'd say they weigh at least an ounce if not more. When I'm going after trout with a bubble I generally use a 7 foot spinning rig spooled with 8 pound monofilament. A rig like this teamed with the aerodynamically shaped heft of a water filled bubble adds up to the ability to cast extremely long distances. The further you can cast the more water your lure is going to cover.

You've probably been wondering why I fill the bubble completely full with water? Here's the deal. Sometimes I want to present my offering just a hair below the surface. Other times I'll want to get it down a bit. If there is air in your bubble the bubble is going to float. That's fine if you want to fish just under the surface, but you won't be able to get any depth.

On the other hand a full bubble has zero buoyancy. If you allow a full bubble to set in one spot without retrieving it, it will slowly sink and you can count it down. When using flies teamed with a full bubble a deadly trick is to stop your retrieve periodically and allow the bubble to sink, slowly drawing the fly down with it. Lots of times the sight of that slowly descending fly is tempting enough to turn followers into hooked fish.

When I rig up for bubble fishing I use a reel spooled with standard high quality mono, but I use 6 or 8 pound fluorocarbon for my leader. I've used leaders as long as 5 feet and as short as 18 inches. Overall I think leaders in the 24 to 36 inch range work best. These leaders are long enough to get the bait away from the bubble a bit, but not so long as to make casting difficult.

When targeting trout the number one offering you can employ is a streamer style fly that incorporates marabou. My favorites are either woolly buggers or Sep's trolling flies. Big flies will catch fish, but if big flies fail don't be afraid to go smaller and smaller until you get hit. In high mountain lakes I've found No. 14 and 16 aquatic beetle imitations to be deadly.

In addition to flies you can employ a variety of tiny spoons like the afore mentioned Dick Nites and Sockeye Slammers as well as Sep's Pro Secrets.

Natural baits like mealworms, whole threaded night crawlers, pieces of threaded crawler, crickets and Pautzke salmon eggs also work great when teamed with a bubble.

Now that you've got some ideas about what to throw let's talk presentation. As a general rule bubble fishing means using a slow seductive retrieve. Most of the time you want to make a long cast and then S-L-O-W-L-Y retrieve the rig.

A full bobber makes a substantial splash when it hits the water and you might be worried that the splash will scare the trout. I used to worry about that, but over time I've come to believe that the splash actually attracts trout.

I generally start out working my full bubble just under the surface. I cast and immediately start my retrieve after splash down. I elevate the rod tip a bit and make my retrieve so I can just see the submerged bubble bulging the surface. The wake the bubble creates also seems to draw fish close. When they come to investigate and spot that fly it's often Fish On!

When steady near surface retrieves aren't working, I'll experiment with pauses and twitches and I'll try counting the bubble down to various depths.

Strikes don't tend to be savage or super subtle either. The small slow moving offerings typically used look like an easy meal to the trout. As a result they just seem to cruise up behind flies and small lures and engulf them.

Generally when you get hit you'll feel weight, but sometimes you'll feel a harder grab. Regardless you want to use a hook set that I refer to as a load up set. Instead of simply rearing back on the rod, I start my hookset with several fast cranks of the reel. Only when the tip of the rod starts to load against the fish do I come back with the rod and rather than using a sharp jab, I use more of a sweep to imbed the hook deeply.

More often than not when using the hook setting approach I've outlined you'll find that the hook is imbedded right in the corner of the trout's mouth. The flesh and cartridge in that area is tough and there is little danger of the fish shaking the hook.

Chapter Seven: So Now You Want A Boat?

Summer is in full swing and the lake's surface temperature has crept into the upper 70's. Back in the days when you fished from the bank exclusively, a trip up to a cool high mountain lake would have been necessary to find trout within casting distance of the shoreline, but that's not the case anymore. These days you have a new boat.

After sliding your new toy off the trailer, you put up the canvass top to block the sun, crack open a cold soda and motor off toward some deep narrows about 6 miles away. A short time later you slow the boat as it glides into the narrows and begin watching the sonar unit intently. Almost immediately the fish finder's screen lights up with big spikes of bait and larger fish holding from 45 to 65 feet deep.

After quickly deploying your remote control driven electric trolling motor you rig a light rod with a dodger trailing a small spoon with fingers made clumsy from adrenaline. After free spooling the rig out behind the boat you clip it to the portside downrigger and send it down to 60 feet. Finally you clip a 3 foot dropper also armed with a light spoon to the main line, knowing it will drop down and work near the 30 foot mark.

You've only been trolling for about two minutes when the line pops off the downrigger and begins pulsing violently. Grabbing the rod, you begin fighting the first trout of the day. Seconds later the rod loads up even more and the sharp tugs you had been feeling are replaced with dead weight and muted surges

Confused you continue working the reel while standing close to the net, ready for whatever emerges from the depths. At long last a husky 2 pound rainbow materializes below the portside corner and then you spot a second fish. You've been fishing less than 5 minutes and you've got a double header! As near as you can tell you hooked the first rainbow on the lure working behind the dodger and as that fish came up one of his twin buddies latched onto the dropper. What a way to kick off a day of trout fishing!

Bank fishing is exciting and productive, there's no doubt about that, but piloting your own boat takes things to a new level. A boat gives you a wonderful sense of freedom. You can troll, cast, drift or anchor and soak bait. You can fish shallow or deep, close to shore or out in the middle of the lake. Do you think trout are holding down by the dam? Well, run over there and check it out. Maybe they are holding up in the river arm where the water is cool? You're just a turn of the key or a pull of the starter rope from finding out.

Quite a few trout anglers are like me. I started out fishing from the bank exclusively and it didn't take me long to become pretty good at establishing patterns and catching trout. Wanting more range and mobility, I eventually graduated up to 12 foot Gregor. At first the only means of propulsion I had was an electric trolling motor. My next acquisition was a 15 horse Honda outboard. These days I cruise around in a 20 foot heavy aluminum boat powered by a 90 horse Mercury outboard. My boat sports most of the standard bells and whistles popular with guides and hardcore trout enthusiasts.

Choosing a boat is a highly personal decision, but we can examine some basic boat styles and options that will make any boat you choose as functional as possible. Back in the days when I fished exclusively out of my 12 foot Gregor I caught a lot of trout, but I wasn't very comfortable while catching them. The boat didn't have a canvas top and as a result I soaked in the rain and fried in the sun. Due to the boat's size, moving around was pretty much impossible. After a day of setting in one position I'd get really stiff and my lower back wouldn't recover for a couple days.

Finally as most anglers know, trout lakes are often subject to stiff afternoon winds. While I always tried to anticipate the arrival of the wind and get off the water before it really started kicking up, there were a number of times that I got caught flat footed several miles from the dock. At these times I kept a cool head, tightened the straps on my life jacket and took my time maneuvering through formidable white caps on my way back to the ramp. Such incidents represent a real gut check for the small boater that leave you saying "never again". But of course with time you forget the ride through the whitecaps and sooner or later find yourself idling through rough water once again.

On the positive side, small boats do offer some important advantages and that's why I've kept my little Gregor all these years. First they take up very little storage space at your house. Secondly, they are easy to tow even on the narrow often rutted roads that lead to high country lakes. These days when gas prices seem to go up on a daily basis the small amount of fuel that a 10 or 15 horse motor consumes is a wonderful thing. In my Gregor I can run for miles and troll all day long on 4 or 5 gallons of unleaded. Small boats are also a lot more budget friendly as compared to big top of the line craft. Three or four thousand dollars will get you out on the water in a small boat, while a big aluminum trout sled will run from twenty to forty thousand dollars depending on the type of motor you choose.

Big boats in the 18 to 22 foot range are an absolute pleasure to fish from. They are stable and literally eat up rough water. Large craft provide ample elbow room for walking around and fighting fish. Storage space is plentiful, so you don't have to waste a lot of preparation time loading tackle into the boat when it's time to go fishing. Large boats typically come equipped with canvass tops and plastic side curtains that keep you cool in the summer and dry in the winter. Add a small propane heater and you'll stay cozy in even the coldest weather. Toss an inflatable mattress and sleeping bag aboard and you'll be able to stay out on the boat for an entire weekend.

The negatives as they relate to big boats pretty much contrast the positives that small boats offer. Large boats require a substantial investment. They burn quite a bit of fuel. Towing them over rough dirt roads isn't wise and you've got to set aside a fairly large chunk of your garage, driveway or backyard to store them.

All things considered, I believe you should buy the largest boat you can comfortably afford. I've know too many folks, including myself that have invested in a small boat only to go out and get a larger one a few months or years later. If price is an issue, consider buying a used boat. This way you can beat the depreciation curve and get the most for your hard earned cash. If you go the used route be sure to have the boat's motor checked out by a reliable marine mechanic before making a commitment.

One of the first decisions that the perspective boat buyer must consider is the construction of the hull. Aluminum and fiberglass are the two basic materials used for building hulls. Both offer advantages and disadvantages. These days most anglers opt for aluminum construction. Aluminum is strong and light in weight. An aluminum hull's lightness translates into a high ratio of speed to engine horsepower and great fuel efficiency. The lightweight of aluminum sleds also make for easy towing and less wear and tear on the tow vehicle.

There are two primary knocks against aluminum hulls. First of all they offer no insulation, which means that the chill of the water travels right through the metal. Setting at home in the easy chair this doesn't sound important, but when you're out on the lake on a cold stormy day it starts to take on more meaning.

The second drawback may not be a drawback at all depending on your perspective. The strength and lightweight of aluminum boats means that they are rigid, light and speedy. In choppy conditions aluminum hulls easily hammer their way across the top of the water. At this point in my fishing career I love the pounding and the adrenaline rush of catching air when I hit big rollers. A few years from now, when I'm older and mellower this might not be the case.

Guys that choose fiberglass hulls generally do so because of the comfortable ride. Fiberglass is heavy. A fiberglass hull doesn't bounce across the surface chop. Instead it smashes through it resulting in a much smoother ride as compared to an aluminum sled. A secondary benefit of fiberglass is that it provides better insulation than aluminum. Fiberglass doesn't conduct the cold efficiently and you feel warmer on those miserable cold days.

The drawbacks of fiberglass are mainly related to its weigh. Fiberglass hulls require more horsepower to push them through the water as compared to a similar size aluminum boat, which results in lower fuel efficiency and higher operating costs. These costs are also passed on to the tow vehicle in reduced gas mileage and stress on the vehicle's engine and transmission.

Today aluminum and fiberglass boats sell for comparable prices, but this could change drastically in the future. Aluminum prices have risen significantly over the past few years. If that trend continues the cost of aluminum boats could go up substantially. If and when that happens more and more fiberglass trout boats will undoubtedly begin appearing on lakes.

I only want to make one point about selecting a motor for your boat. The motor is the most expensive single component of a boat in nearly every case. For this reason a lot of guys try to save money when it comes time to pick out a motor. They typically do this by purchasing the bare minimum in terms of horsepower.

Under calm conditions while operating at a low elevation a marginally powerful motor will likely push the boat along at an acceptable pace, but this is not the true test of a motor. When you've got to make a long run into high wind and frothy white caps, you want as much power as you can get. This isn't to imply that you'll be running at full tilt under these conditions, but you'll need extra power to push through the rollers and to keep the boat's bow down as much as possible.

When you take your boat to a high elevation lake you'll notice a substantial loss of gitty-up. Now if you are a mechanical type, which I am not, you can adjust the air to fuel ratio and get that power back. If you are like me, you'll just have to live with the loss of power. If your motor was marginally adequate down at sea level, you won't have the power you need at higher elevations. I live at about 1,000 feet in elevation. My boat runs at about 38 miles per hour at a lake just outside the town where I live. One of my favorite lakes is situated at about 4,800 feet. When I tow the boat up there my top speed drops to about 30 miles per hour, illustrating the difference a 3,800 foot climb in elevation can make.

The trout angler's boat represents both a means of transportation to and from the fishing grounds as well as a platform to fish from. The better outfitted the boat is the more efficient it will be as a fishing platform. An electric trolling motor is a good place to begin the quest for accessories. An electric motor offers quiet power that enables stealthy low speed trolling. For a small boat in the 12 to 14 foot range a manually operated transom mounted model works just fine. For larger boats a bow mounted model is the best choice.

Most electrics designed for bow mounting come equipped with a foot peddle control that allows you to steer and power the boat from a distance using your foot. The bow mounted Minn Kota that is on my boat currently, gives me the option of controlling it using a foot peddle or I can opt to use a hand held remote. The remote is less than 2 inches long. It can be attached to the butt of a fishing rod, my wrist or worn around the neck. For me using the remote took a little bit of getting used to, but at this point I wouldn't be without one. I tend to fish alone quite a bit and it allows me to easily maintain control of the boat while rigging tackle or fighting trout. Units that incorporate a hand held remote cost more than models that only utilize a foot peddle, but I can attest that those extra dollars are well spent.

Moving up the ladder in terms of convenience and cost, programmable electric motors are available. These motors will steer a steady course and the best units will steer a course from waypoint to waypoint. If your wallet is fat, these high-tech self-steering motors make a day on the water even better because they allow you to focus on fishing, not on steering, speed control and fighting the breeze.

Now that we've touched on both gas and electric propulsion there are two more accessories that are absolutely essential. I'm talking about a sonar unit and a set of downriggers. Sonar is a must have tool for almost all modern day anglers whether they are targeting trout or blue water battlers such as marlin. Not only does sonar give the advantage of being able to identify fish, but it also lets you see the contours of the bottom and this is often key in predicting where fish will be found.

There are a myriad of different sonar units on the market being produced by companies such as Lowrance, Furuno, Humminbird and Garmin to name only four. Being an outdoor writer I'm in the unique position to see units from almost every manufacturer in action on the water. For what it's worth the majority of guides employ units made by Lowrance or Furuno while a few rely on Humminbird. From an effectiveness and reliability standpoint I don't think there is much difference between the various manufacturers.

The most important thing when it comes to purchasing a unit is to do your homework and get the unit that is best suited for your style of fishing. I chase most species of fish so I need an upper end unit that offers me ample speed and power to spot fish in deep water when the boat is moving along at a good clip. If I were only chasing trout in lakes and reservoirs, I could probably get by with a midrange unit in terms of price.

In general what you are looking for in a trout fishing unit is plenty of power and a wide dual sonar beam. A dual beam system that features something in the neighborhood of a 60 degree area of coverage offers the ability to show great definition when it comes to scanning structure and bottom contours in addition to spotting fish. You'll also want to make sure that the unit you're interested in monitors and displays the water temperature.

Some sonar units come teamed with a Global Positioning Satellite system or GPS. Naturally these units cost more, but if you have the money they are worth the price. GPS allows you to both navigate in poor weather conditions and darkness as well as the ability to mark key areas or the position of fish holding in open water. Finally a GPS unit allows you to accurately monitor your ground speed and this is very important when trolling.

If you are a hunter as well as an angler you can save a few bucks by picking up a hand held GPS unit. This way you can buy a cheaper sonar unit without GPS and you can use your versatile hand held unit while both fishing and hunting.

When you think about it, a downrigger is really a pretty simple piece of equipment. It's basically a big spool full of cable teamed with a short boom, employed for the purpose of lowering a heavy weight down to a desired depth and up again. When it comes to buying a downrigger the question becomes how do you want to accomplish this task and how much money do you want to spend?

If you are on a budget you can go with manual crank models. If money is not a concern, automatic electric units are convenient and efficient. As with sonar units there are a number of different downrigger manufacturers. If you are going with manual units there is not much difference which major manufacturer you choose, since they are all well made and reliable. On the other hand if you choose to purchase electric downriggers, I would go with Cannons or Scottys.

Cannon offers downriggers with positive ion control, meaning that they put off positive fish attracting electrical current into the water. In terms of electric Cannon downriggers there are currently several successively more expensive units to choose from ranging from the Magnum 5 ST at the lower end and the Digi Troll 10 at the upper end.

The difference between these units comes down to the bells and whistles. The Magnum 5 ST basically goes up and down with the flick of a switch, while dispensing positive current into the water. The Digi Troll offers things like programmable descent and retrieval rates, adjustable ion control and the ability to team the unit with a depth finder for bottom tracking such as when trolling for mackinaw.

In 1952 Blayney and his wife Almeda Scott started a small company in Victoria, British Columbia, Canada that pioneered the use of plastics in the manufacturing of salmon fishing lures and other marine products.

From humble beginnings, Scott Plastics Ltd. has evolved to produce thousands of products under the Scotty Trademark which are sold into the fishing, marine, outdoor and firefighting industries worldwide.

Scotty produces a full line of products, yet when most of us hear the name Scotty we think of quality downriggers, and why not? Scotty has been producing some of the finest manual and electric downriggers that money can buy for decades.

As reliable as the last generation of Scotty electric downriggers were, Scotty raised the stakes recently when they unveiled their new line of High Performance electric downriggers.

"We've got 60 years of experience under our belts and we put all the knowledge we've accumulated to work in our new High Performance downriggers," related Scotty's Bill Emile. "The reliability of our new units has been very good. These downriggers were designed with the heavy weights and extreme depths of saltwater trolling in mind. We know that when we field a downrigger that stands up to the challenges of fishing saltwater, that it will easily handle the challenges of fishing freshwater. "

The list of features and attributes that Scotty's High Performance downriggers offer is extensive and it starts with speed. The fastest retrieval rates in the world! For example if you rig up for ocean salmon with a 20 pound ball, it will come up at a blazing fast rate of 260 feet per minute!

The downriggers come spooled with 300 feet of 180 pound test wire. The belts that drive the downrigger are a half inch wide and constructed out of Kevlar. All the downrigger's hardware is corrosion resistant and every one of them is load tested at the factory.

The list goes on and on, but suffice to say if you want to outfit your boat with fast reliable downriggers, Scotty's new

High Performance downriggers will get the job done. They are offered in three different sizes to meet the needs of all anglers.

Chapter Eight: Getting Them On The Troll

In the flat lands far below, the grind of the morning commute would just be getting underway and lucky for me I wasn't going to be part of it...That was my thought as I put the last of the gear into the boat. The sound of aluminum groaning against gravel sounded loud and alien as I shoved the boat away from the bank and jumped in. Expectations always run high at the beginning of a fishing adventure, but this day promised to be especially memorable.

Less than two weeks before the lake had been covered with a thin shell of ice and the remnants of snowdrifts had made the access road nearly impassable. The lake had only been fished a handful of times since the previous November. I was confident that its rainbows and browns would be plenty hungry and very willing to cooperate.

With overcast skies and a steady breeze whipping up a low chop, the conditions couldn't have been any better. After making a two mile run down to the area where the overflow channel bypassed the dam I killed the gas motor and switched over to the electric. I set up one rod with a chrome and blue Cripplure and was in the process of rigging my second rod with a small Yo-Zuri minnow plug when my peripheral vision caught movement on the bank. My first reaction was that I was looking at a black Labrador Retriever, but as soon as my brain had a moment to compute I realized that it was a smallish black bear that had absolutely no idea anyone was around. I watched he bear for several minutes before it finally drifted out of sight into the dark timber.

Just seeing the bear had made the trip a success whether I caught fish or not. Getting down to business, I finished rigging the second rod, put some herring scent on the lures, free spooled them back about two hundred feet behind the boat and put the rods in their holders. The plan was to troll past the mouth of the overflow channel and then zig zag back and forth along the dam's rip rap, but I didn't get very far. The lures had been in the water for five minutes at the longest when the rod sporting the Cripplure on the portside got hammered.

The trout immediately began ripping line off the reel and there was so much strain on the rod that I had trouble getting it out of the holder. Freeing the rod I started fighting the fish while simultaneously circling the boat back out over deep water. I'd been enjoying the slashing runs of the trout for a minute or so when a husky rainbow rocketed out of the water off the starboard corner. Initially I thought it was the trout I was fighting, but a beat later I saw the second rod pulsing and realized that I had a double header.

I worked as quickly as I could to get the fish on the first rod within net range, but before I could the trout on the second rod made another wild jump and I knew there was a pretty good chance it would shake the hook. By the time I slid the first holdover into the net the line on the second rod had gone completely slack. After giving the first rainbow a love tap with the fish billy, I grabbed rod number two and started reeling up the loose line. I'd probably retrieved about a hundred feet of slack when the line suddenly became tight against the weight of a hefty fish. Having already expended a good deal of energy, the second trout was determined to stay deep. Every time I gained a few feet of line the trout would move off slowly taking back the line I'd earned. In the end the resilience of the rod won out and the thick bodied trout wallowed to the surface.

What a morning! It had been light for less than an hour and I already had a pair of handsome rainbows pushing the 3 pound mark in the cooler. For the next four hours I experienced some of the most exciting trolling of my life as rainbow after rainbow pounced on my lures. By the time lunch rolled around I'd landed two dozen trout and filled out my five fish limit with a second double hook up.

Trolling is the most exciting and efficient tactic a trout angler can use, yet it is also one of the most misunderstood and misused approaches. Many beginning anglers and even some veterans oversimplify trolling and view the technique as little more than dragging a randomly selected lure around behind the boat. When trout are aggressive, willing to chase and holding near the surface like they were on the morning I just described, trolling is a no brainer and virtually anyone pulling a lure behind their boat will catch fish. If trout are holding in deep water, inactive or sluggish, trolling can get a whole lot tougher, leaving anglers that don't have a thorough understanding of trolling saying, "Well, I guess they just ain't bite'n..."

I used to be one of those guys that looked at trolling as a simplistic approach that required little in the way of technique. As a result my success rate was strictly hit and miss, but that isn't the case anymore.

Several years ago I met Gary Miralles of the Shasta Tackle Company and a great friendship quickly developed. Gary's name is prominent among west coast trout fishing aficionados.

Gary is a lifelong trout angler that began designing lures during his teenage years. In 1988 his hobby became his vocation. That year he founded the Shasta Tackle Company and started manufacturing trout tackle on a full time basis. These day's Gary's innovative gear holds a number of patents and he has risen through the ranks to become one of the west's most respected trout and land locked salmon guides.

My interactions with Gary have had a profound impact on the way I approach trolling. I now view trolling as a systematic strategy that allows me to quickly gage the temperament and activity level of the trout. When Gary heads out for a day on the water the first thing he does is access what type of forage is available to the trout. At most foothill reservoirs the primary forage is open water baitfish in the form of threadfin shad or Japanese pond smelt. At higher elevation lakes chubs and aquatic insects are often the primary foods of the trout. At certain times when the conditions are right trout will feed heavily on small freshwater shrimp, while ignoring both baitfish and insects.

 Once you've got an idea of what the trout at a given lake are feeding on this information should dictate the size and color of the lures you employ. Obviously, when the trout are feeding on baitfish it is important to match the size and shape of the lure to the available bait, but what about color?

Color selection is one of the areas where Gary and I disagree to some extent. When it comes to imitating baitfish, Gary is of the opinion that you should vary the color of your baitfish imitating lures based on depth and the color spectrum. "When choosing lure colors consider the rainbow. Red is the top color followed by orange, yellow, green, blue and finally purple. Near the top of the water column reds and oranges are highly visible. As you descend in depth yellows and greens stand out well. In deep water, blue and purple patterns are the most vivid colors," Gary asserts.

I advocate a match the hatch philosophy in terms of imitating baitfish regardless of the depth. While matching the silvers, greens and blues that baitfish exhibit is important, imitating the dark and light contrasts they exhibit is equally important. Baitfish are dark above and light below, this is a color scheme that trout are accustomed to seeing and I believe lures that match this contrast trigger more strikes. Since trout feed on baitfish and baitfish don't change colors as they move into deeper water I don't vary lure color much as I drop down in the water column. Chrome/blue, blue/white, black/white and purple/chrome are among my favorite lure color combinations for imitating shad and pond smelt.

In situations where the trout are feeding on shrimp, plankton, aquatic insects or chubs, you're not in a position to match the hatch with trolled lures. In these instances, you've got to change your focus from matching the forage of the trout, to presenting them with an offering that will trigger a reaction strike, either out of curiosity or aggression. Gary and I agree that this is best accomplished by using brightly colored highly visible lures. Red, orange, chartreuse, hot pink and firetiger are colors that really shine for triggering reaction bites. These same colors are good when dealing with stained murky water or when fishing during periods of low light.

One of the things that distinguishes Gary from a lot of other trollers is that he prefers to troll quickly, only slowing down when he has to. This philosophy is reflected in two of Gary's marquee lures, the Hum Dinger and the Cripplure. When you head out to the lake you are going to either be confronted with active or inactive trout. Active trout are typically feeding fish that are willing to chase a lure. Inactive trout are not in a feeding mode and in order to draw strikes from them you've got to present them with a lure that moves erratically and stays in the strike zone as long as possible.

The Hum Dinger, like the Kastmaster, Needlefish and Excel to name only a few are slim profile spoons that are best trolled at a brisk pace from 2 to 2. 5 miles per hour. Cripplures, Super Dupers and Sep's Pro Secrets are bulkier lures that provide a lot of action and create a great deal of vibration when trolled slowly, say from . 75 to 1. 5 miles per hour. When the going gets tough and it is time to slow down, the Cripplure is my all-time favorite lure. It has a one of a kind erratic rolling action that milks strikes out of the most inactive trout.

A sound basic strategy when going out for a day on the water is to assume that the trout are actively feeding and begin covering various levels of the water column quickly with lures that work well at relatively high speeds. If the fish are in an active state they will let you know it in short order. If you don't get hit while moving quickly don't get discouraged. The trout are simply telling you that they aren't feeling too energetic. Start slowing down gradually, until you begin getting some action.

So far I've only been talking about spoons. While spoons represent the heart and soul of the trout trollers arsenal there are some other must have lures that should be present in every serious angler's tackle selection. Spinners have been mainstay offerings with trout trollers for decades. Traditional style spinners that are constructed on a piece of wire such as Panther Martins, Roostertails, Mepps and Blue Foxes can be highly effective, yet these days a new generation of spinners that are constructed on a monofilament leader such as Uncle Larry's Spinners are much more popular among the trolling fraternity. While these new generation spinners will take trout when fished alone, they are even more effective when tipped with a piece of worm, salmon eggs or even PowerBait.

Plugs represent another important component of a well prepared troller's lure selection. The Rapala floating minnow plug is a traditional favorite of trout anglers the world over. For many years floating Rapalas constructed of balsa wood were really the only plugs used by trout anglers. While the regal Rapala remains every bit as effective as it was in days gone by, over the past several years a number of lures have arrived on the trout fishing scene that rival the Rapala both in terms of quality and effectiveness. I continue to use traditional floating Rapalas on a regular basis, but I also employ minnow plugs and small crankbaits from Yo-Zuri and Lucky Craft. These baits make use of high quality components, feature extremely life like finishes and run true right out of the box.

For general use you'll want minnow plugs that range from 1. 5 to 3 inches in length. This corresponds to Rapalas in sizes F5 and F7. Yo-Zuri Pin Minnows in size No. F196 and the Hardcore Jerk in size No. F684. The Lucky Craft Pointer No. PT65 and PT 78 along with the Deep Pointer in sizes No. 65DD and 78DD are great baits if you don't mind spending a few extra dollars. Your minnow plug assortment doesn't need to feature a wide variety of colors schemes. I get by nicely with just a few such as, rainbow trout, black over silver, firetiger and bright orange.

In addition to slim profile minnow plugs, I also carry a few broad profile crankbaits such as the Rapala Shad Rap in the

No. SR5 size, Yo-Zuri's 3D Flat Crank in the No. F683 size, small Hotshots or the Shasta Tackle Flee Bitty. These lures display the same bulky profile of crankbaits intended for bass fishing, but in a smaller package. The broad profile and wiggling action these plugs display make them very effective when trout are feeding on shad. Once again you don't need a big selection of these baits in terms of color. If you have a model that imitates the dark above light below color scheme of a baitfish and a bright pattern such as firetiger, you'll be well prepared.

Apex Lures or Pro Troll's Trout Killers are hybrid lures that remind me of a cross between a spoon and a plug. These lures have a solid following among trollers and many guides use them extensively for targeting both trout and salmon. Monte Smith of Gold Country Guide Service, one of California's most talented trout and salmon guides, swears by the effectiveness of Apex Lures.

"The Apex is a great lure for rainbows, browns and kokanee salmon. When I'm using it for 'kokes I usually run it 24 inches behind a dodger, but when I'm after trout I fish it alone," says Smith. "One of the things I really like about the Apex is its versatility. It is a lure that can be trolled fast or slow, deep or shallow and they come in a bunch of different colors. Early and late in the day or when working really deep water I particularly like the U. V. patterns. During the middle of the day, the U. V. finishes are effective, but I think standard finishes work just as well. When the bite is tough an effective trick is to slide an Apex off its leader, reverse it and slid it back on. When trolled backwards these lures have a wild erratic action that can trigger strikes from hard to catch heavily pressured fish. "

Mike McNeilly is an accomplished trout angler and regular contributor to the Fish Sniffer Magazine. Here's what he had to say about Apex Lures and Trout Killers.

"I don't believe Apexs and Trout Killers mimic any one forage item in particular. If I had to hypothesize, they most likely resemble a minnow that has been mortally wounded and is swimming erratically. Be that as it may, they work very well in fisheries where the fish spend most of their time eating invertebrates. In fisheries like Crowley Lake, trout spend most of their time feeding on aquatic insects and small crustaceans. Yet, they will pounce on a quickly trolled Trout Killer or Apex.

My conclusion is that the action of the lure elicits the strike. Ideally, the proper action of one of these lures should be a constant wobble similar to a Flatfish, followed by the whole lure rolling over once in a while. If you are getting the wobble without the roll, you are going too slow, and if the lure is constantly rolling you are going too fast. "

"**So which lure is better,** the original the Apex made by Hotspot, or the Trout Killer made by Pro Troll? I own both variations, and sometimes it has come down to which lure was available in the color I wanted. Both lures have caught fish for me, but the Trout Killer does feature an E-Chip that may be the cherry on top of the fish catching sundae. The Trout Killer also can be trolled slightly faster than the Apex, and it comes with better hooks out of the box. I would suggest you buy both makes and start throwing them in your rotation of trolling lures. You will likely be impressed with the violent strikes and surprisingly large trout these lures will produce," added McNeilly.

Lures are only part of the picture in terms of the end tackle needed for trout trolling. You'll also need some attractors in the form of dodgers and flashers. A dodger is a thin piece of metal that kicks back and forth when drawn through the water. Dodgers come in a variety of colors, sizes and designs. On the front of the dodger you'll find a swivel where the mainline from the rod is attached. A snap swivel is attached to the rear of the dodger where the leader and lure are attached. Flashers are a series of 3 to 5 spinner blades attached to a section of light cable. As with the dodger there is a swivel on the front of the cable where the main line is attached and a snap swivel at the rear for connecting a leader and lure.

Dodgers basically do three things. They create vibration and flash. And they can impart an erratic surging motion to lures and baits, depending on how far you rig them behind the dodger.

It is thought that the vibration put off by dodgers is similar to those put off by feeding fish. Fish like trout and salmon have a strip of nerves along the lateral line that allow them to pick up and analyze vibrations in the water around them.

When the lateral line picks up vibrations that sound like fish feeding, predatory gamefish, being the opportunists they are home in on the sound hoping to pick up an easy meal. When they move in on the vibrations put out by a dodger and see your lure, they grab it.... That's the plan anyway!

While I think that vibration is the driving factor behind a dodger's ability to create strikes, you can't discount the fish attracting value of flash either.

For a long time I used to wonder just how much flash a dodger could possibly produce. One early morning not that long ago, I was heading out to meet my fishing partner hours before dawn for a day of kokanee trolling. I had several pre-rigged rods leaning in the front passengers seat of my truck.

As I approached an intersection where there were a handful of cars moving in different directions there was a sudden bright flash that I swear illuminated the entire cab of the truck. My eyes were adjusted to the dark and it was almost as if a flash bulb had gone off. Looking around I realized that the beam of another vehicle's headlights had hit the chrome surface of a 4-inch dodger attached to one of the rods. That incident left no doubt in my mind as to the ability of even a small dodger to create flash significant enough to draw fish in from many yards away. Conversely in the wrong situation they can also throw off enough flash to scare fish too, but we'll get into that a little later.

Dodgers come in a variety of styles and sizes. "Herring Dodgers" are oval shaped on either end, have an upswept edge at either end and a uniform width. A lot of companies market a line of herring style dodgers. Familiar names include Vance's Tackle, Sep's Pro Fishing, Luhr Jensen, Worden's Lures, Mack's Lures and Gold Star. Some of these models are made out of thicker metal than others. This of course makes them heavier and they run deeper than thinner lighter models.

Another popular style of dodger is the thin or tapered dodger. The Shasta Tackle Sling Blade sets the standard in this type of dodger. Sling Blades are larger at the rear than they are at the front and they have a constant taper throughout their length. These dodgers only have an upswept edge at the rear end.

You should be aware of a third type of dodger that a lot of folks refer to as mini dodgers. Popular examples of these dodgers include the Sep's Side Kick and Sep's Strike Master along with the Crystal Basin Wild Thing. These dodgers are basically teardrop shape and cupped at the rear end. The Side Kick is 2 inches long while both the Strike Master and the Wild Thing are 3 inches long.

Herring dodgers can typically be found in 4, 5 6 and 8 inch sizes, while Sling Blades come in 4, 6 and 8-inch version. I've caught both salmon and trout while running big 8-inch dodgers, but in most situations you'll be best served with dodgers in the 4, 5 and 6-inch class. Having said that you should have all three types of dodgers I've described including mini dodgers in your tackle assortment to cover all the variables you are likely to encounter out on the water.

When fishing for trout I start out with 4-inch dodgers and they usually do the trick. Once in a while I'll break out a 6-inch dodger when targeting these species. I think that larger dodgers can give you an edge when working deep water.

Now that we've gone over the basic styles of dodgers available, it's time to think about dodger color.

Dodger color is confusing to a lot of anglers. Dodgers come in about as many color schemes as lures. Common questions include, what colors are best? How many different colors do I need? And do I need to match lure color with dodger color?

The first question is a sucker's bet. There is no best color, as it's the light level, water depth and water clarity that dictate the best color for a given day.

As to how many colors you need, the simple answer is that collecting dodgers gets addictive and you'll surely end up with a lot more color schemes than you actually need! Dodgers are something you don't lose too often, so it's pretty easy to end up with 50 or more of them after a few years of just buying one here and there.

Finally as far as matching lure color to dodger color goes, some guys I know are very careful about doing this while others pay no attention to it at all. I'm in the no attention at all camp.

While I've got a bunch of dodgers and certainly catch my share of trout and salmon, I'm no expert. This being the case, I picked up the phone and called up a pair of the most knowledgeable guys I know when it comes to trout and salmon gear and put the color question to them.

My first call was to Vance Staplin of Vance's Tackle Company. He's been manufacturing dodgers and guiding for many years, so his observations carry a good deal of weight.

"Color means a lot, but it's really the conditions that dictate dodger color," Vance related. "Early in the day when light level is low, you want flash. So chrome is a good choice as are glow models. When the light level increases you'll typically benefit from toning down on flash. When the sun is high and the water is clear the intense flashing of a chrome dodger can actually scare fish away. You can tone down your spread by swapping your chrome dodgers for copper, brass and painted models. "

"Everyone has colors and color combinations that they have a lot of confidence in. You want to keep an open mind. Make logical color choices, but really let the fish tell you what they want. Having said that, there are colors that really work well for a given species. For example, when I'm targeting rainbows I almost always have something green or chartreuse in the water, simply because that color has proven itself for me so many times," added Vance.

My next call was to Gary Miralles of the Shasta Tackle Company. Gary like Vance is a tackle manufacturer with a ton of experience and he too is a well-respected guide. Gary's line of Sling Blade dodgers are well known and have put a bunch of big fish in the box over the years including the current world record kokanee.

"For me more than anything else dodger color is about depth and the light level," Gary related. "When I pick out a dodger I think about the depths I'm fishing and the color spectrum. Colors disappear as you descend in the water column. Up top your reds and oranges show up well. In the middle depths greens work well for me and when I really drop down deep where light penetration is minimized I like blues, glows and of course UV. When I'm fishing for trout up near the surface during stormy weather or anytime the light level is really low, I tend to lean toward darker colored dodgers. I think a darker color creates a more distinct silhouette for trout looking up toward the surface. "

Depth, light level, water clarity, light penetration and on and on. You can think and rethink everything when it comes to fishing and one fact remains constant, fish love to break the rules and seem to get a kick out of driving us anglers crazy! With that in mind I'm going to toss out a few colors that I've found to be very consistent producers a lot of the time.

I've had great luck running chrome and green, chrome and blue and watermelon colored dodgers for trout, particularly rainbows. To my knowledge I don't think I've encountered a situation where rainbows are put off by excessive flash.

When it comes to kokanee I've done very well with chrome and green, watermelon, bright orange, pink and glow models. Kokanee can absolutely be put off by too much flash. For 'kokes I start off bright early and then as the day goes on switch over to coppers. I've caught lots of kokanee on pink, watermelon and UV Sling Blades, chrome/green and copper/pink Vance's Dodgers and Sep's dodgers in glow/orange stripe and watermelon.

For landlocked kings I've had good luck with chromes, pinks, UV and glows. Kings seem to like plain Jane chrome dodgers just as much as they do the wild looking stuff. When it comes to crazy colors and kings, I've had a good deal of luck with the Sep's UV fruit salad color.

One last thing I should touch on before turning my attention to rigs is trolling speed. When you are trolling with dodgers you want to be moving fast enough to cause the dodger to dance back and forth, but not so fast as to make the dodger flip over and spin. Of course the best way to determine the best speed for a given dodger is to put it in the water right beside the boat and match the boat speed to the best action of the dodger.

Herring style dodgers offer aggressive action at low speeds. As a general rule most small herring dodgers will start spinning at around 1. 8 miles per hour. On the other hand slim Sling Blade style dodgers don't offer real aggressive action at low speed. They typically perform best from 1. 8 to 2. 5 or even 3 miles per hour.

Mini dodgers behave much like herring dodgers in that slow is the way to go. Much more speed than 1. 7 or 1. 8 and they start to roll.

Okay some dodgers work better fast while other perform well at slow speeds. There are a couple tricks you can employ to make Sling Blade style dodgers work better at low speeds and to keep herring style dodgers from spinning when trolled faster than 1. 8.

If you take a Sling Blade out of the package and put it in the water at 1. 5 mph it will have a pretty subtle back and forth wobble. To make it really kick at this sluggish speed, take the blade in your hands with the face side up. Pushing upward with your thumbs work your way up and down the blade and bend a slight arch into it. The more arch you bend into the blade the more action it will have. Use careful measured pressure and test the dodger to see how the action of the blade changes. When it comes time to use the blade for fast trolling again, you can simply bend it back to its original shape.

Split shot is the remedy for a herring dodger that rolls when trolled too fast. While observing a blade working beside the boat figure out the speed where it wants to spin. Pull the blade out of the water and place a split shot on the leader immediately behind the snap on the rear of the dodger. The additional weigh will help to tame the rear of the dodger and it will maintain its kicking motion rather than rolling. The more weight you add the faster you can go to a point. You won't extend the speed range a great deal, but you should be able to break the 2 mph barrier.

When you find yourself out on the water and it's time to rig up, there are only two types of lures to choose from, lures with built in action like spoons, spinners and plugs and lures that produce no action of their own like hoochies and flies.

Lures with no action need to be rigged closed enough to the dodger such that the dodger imparts a surging dart ahead motion to them. As a basic rule you want to position these types of lures two to three dodger lengths behind the blade. If you are using a 4-inch dodger and fishing a kokanee bug behind it, the bug should be on a leader that is 8 to 12 inches long.

Lures that have action give you more latitude. Some guys say that you want spoons and spinners 4 to 5 dodger lengths behind the blade, but other guys use much longer leaders than that. When targeting trout with Hum Dingers and Cripplures trolled behind Sling Blades, Gary Miralles often runs leaders in the 30 to 36 inch range and catches plenty of fish.

The type of lures you are using plays a part in the type of leader material you use. With lures that have action 8-pound test fluorocarbon is about right. 8 pound has enough strength to deal with big strong trout, but it is flexible enough to allow lures to work well.

When using lures without action you want to use heavier stiffer leader line in the 10 to 12 pound range, because stiffer line will transmit more of the action from the dodger to the lure.

In wrapping up this dodger rant, I'll toss out one particular rig that will put a bunch of trout in the boat for you over the course of a year. I knew about this combination for a long time, but it was Monte Smith of Gold Country Guide Service that really illustrated to me how effective it can be.

Monte spends a lot of time fishing at Don Pedro Reservoir. Don Pedro is home to kings, kokanee and trout. Most of the time when Monte takes you out on Pedro the focus is on catching salmon. Monte typically rolls shad deep for kings and runs a couple lines armed with kokanee lures shallower.

This approach covers you for kings and 'kokes, but hanging out above the kokanee, often not far beneath the surface, are the rainbows. Too hook them Monte rigs up a threaded night crawler and trolls it 18 inches to two feet behind a mini dodger. When I first met Monte his dodger of choice for this work was a Sep's Side Kick, but these days he uses the new Sep's Strike Master quite a bit.

I fished with Monte this spring and we caught a bunch of fish on all kinds of different gear. We hooked a pair of rainbows on his Strike Master and worm combo and both of them were dandies. One escaped right behind the boat and the other one ended up in the box comparing notes with a collection of kings and kokanee.

When the going gets tough for trout no matter where you're fishing break out the mini dodgers and worms. This combination will often catch trout when nothing else will.

Flashers also utilize vibration and flash to attract trout, but in a different way than dodgers. Flashers emit high pitched vibrations and small flashes that mimic a school of baitfish. As is the case with dodgers these vibrations are picked up by the trout through their lateral line drawing them within striking distance of your offering. There are a couple of different styles of flashers available. Flashers that utilize oval shaped Colorado blades put off a great deal of vibration, but they also create more resistance when trolled through the water. Slim profile willow leaf blades put off smaller and higher pitched vibrations when compared to Colorado blades, while creating less rod bending resistance. Many different companies produce flashers, but the ones offered by Sep's set the industry standard. In my opinion Sep's small willow leaf flashers and Vance's Slim Willie flashers have no rival. They create plenty of disturbance to pull trout in from a long distance without substantial drag, making them perfect for use with light tackle.

Every year I spend a lot of time top lining for both trout and salmon while using flashers. I catch lots of fish while pulling flashers, but I've noticed something else that is worth mentioning even though it is circumstantial evidence at best...

I've noticed that when I have the flashers in the water, even if that rig isn't getting hit, my partner and I get more hits overall provided we have our other lines working in the top 25 feet of the water column.

When targeting salmon in deepwater trollers often attach ball trolls to their downrigger weights to draw fish into their spread of lures and baits. Could it be that my near surface flashers are doing the same thing, namely pulling fish up toward the top and into a collision course with all the gear behind the boat, not just the lure trailing behind the blades? Flashers definitely pull in and excite fish and when that happens the number of strikes you get should climb on ALL of your gear so long as it is running reasonably close to the blades.

I'm trying to be more observant and with this in mind I've gotten way more strategic about where I position the blades behind the boat. It seems to me that you want them working slightly in front of your other rigs. If our other rigs are running 75 to 100 feet back I'll often strip the flashers out 50 or 60 feet and fish them right off the middle of the stern.

Okay, with a selection of lures in hand that will allow you to target both active and inactive trout, along with a selection of dodgers and a set or two of flashers, there are a few more items you'll need before we can actually get out on the water and begin trolling. A wide range of tackle will work for trolling, but for maximum efficiency and enjoyment you'll want a rod and reel that is matched to the task at hand. For general trolling while top lining or using downriggers a 7 foot light action casting rod rated for 4 to 10 pound test line is the best choice.

There are two schools of thought when it comes to the ideal action for a trolling rod. Some anglers prefer a fast action rod that features a lot of flexibility in the top third of its length near the tip followed up with a stiffer middle and lower section. This is described as a fast action rod with substantial backbone and a sensitive tip. Other anglers like soft slow action rods that develop a parabolic bend from the tip all the way to the handle when a trout is hooked. I have rods in my arsenal that match both of these descriptions. I fish with a lot of different anglers every year with widely varying levels of skill and experience. Personally, like most experienced anglers, I like a rod with some backbone, yet for inexperience anglers I find that they lose less fish when using a soft action stick. Soft action rods are more forgiving than stiffer rods when it comes to pulling hooks out of the soft mouths of hard fighting trout. Whether the rod is constructed of graphite or fiberglass is of little consequence to the troller, since sensitivity is not an important consideration.

The rod should be matched with a high quality level wind baitcasting reel, capable of holding 200 yards of 8 pound test line. The reel should feature a smooth drag and a gear ratio of at least 4 to 1. Some anglers like to use 4 pound test line, while others use line as heavy as 10 pound test. I prefer 8 pound line since it gives me plenty of strength while maintaining a small diameter. Today there a number outstanding lines available to trollers. P-Line and Trilene Maxx are my personal favorites. The most important thing to remember about lines is that you want a quality copolymer line and you want to change it often since all line breaks down and weakens with exposure to sunlight. A couple of the worst things you can do is try to save money by buying bargain line or not changing your line often enough. Both these mistakes cost anglers across the country thousands of big fish each year.

There are a lot of cheap reels on the market these days, but you definitely get what you pay for. The smart angler buys the best reels that they can afford without busting the bank. Quality reels offer smooth drags and durability that translates into years of reliable performance. Over the years I've used reels from just about every manufacturer. In my opinion, Shimano and Abu Garcia produce the best reels available in terms of quality, durability and affordability.

Sure, I know we've been in the tackle store for a long time and the wife is going to kill you when she sees the bill. Since you are already a dead man there are two more things that you'll need. First is a selection of swivels and snap swivels. These little guys are worth their weight in gold since they'll keep your line from getting twisted.

The final component of your trolling tackle arsenal are spools of 6, 8, 10 and 12 pound test fluorocarbon line to use as leader material. The molecular structure of fluorocarbon refracts light in much the same way as water. As a result fluorocarbon is basically invisible when immersed in water. A lot of anglers don't think trout are line shy, but take my word for it when I tell you that in some situations fluorocarbon leaders can mean the difference between catching a limit of fish and getting skunked. This being the case I use fluorocarbon leaders at all times regardless of the situation or conditions.

Perfect! Your wife didn't actually kill, your reels are filled with new line and all the new toys you bought are stashed away in the boat. There's only one thing left to do, put some sandwiches and drinks in an ice chest and head out to the lake. Since you've done your homework, you know what the primary forage at the lake is. If it is a typical west coast reservoir, the trout likely make their living by feeding on either threadfin shad or pond smelt so we'll be using baitfish imitating lures as opposed to the bright stuff we'd likely start out with at a "bug lake".

With the boat in the water the first thing we want to do is turn on the sonar unit and determine what the surface temperature is. Remember the ideal temperature for most trout is 56 degrees. The water temperature gives us a general idea of how deep the trout will be holding. As long as the surface temperature isn't above 68 degrees, there is a good chance that there will be some trout close to the top early in the morning. If the water temperature is in the 50's or lower there will likely be trout in the top 10 feet all day long. As a general guideline the warmer the surface temperature the deeper you will have to go to find the trout.

All right, let's say it is late spring and the surface temperature is 61 degrees when we hit the water. Our first challenge is determining where to begin fishing. If we've fished the lake before or if we made some calls to tackle shops we've likely got some areas in mind that likely hold fish. Assuming we know nothing about the lake and have no preconceived notions it's wise to begin exploring areas based on the terrain. When dealing with a large lake this task is best accomplished with a topographic map. What we are looking for is an area that features structure, points and flats in close proximity to deep water. If you can find an area with these features along with inflowing tributaries you might have stumbled on a true honey hole. I especially like to explore narrow areas such as river arms or bottlenecks between two large bays, since these areas concentrate cruising fish.

Once a promising area is located take the time to cruise around a bit using your sonar to locate some trout or baitfish. If the trout are holding just under the surface you likely won't see them on the sonar because shallow fish tend to move away from the boat before it passes over them. For the sake of this example say that we mark some fish and bait scattered from 15 to 30 feet deep in addition to seeing a couple fish jump. In California where I do most of my fishing each angler has the option of using two rods with a special permit, so let's both rig up a pair of rods.

We are going to assume the trout are feeding. That means we'll be trolling from 2 to 2. 5 miles per hour and we need to choose our lures accordingly. Since the trout are spread out across a variety of depths, we don't want our lures clustered at a single level. Instead we want to spread our offerings out in order to determine which depths are most productive.

On my first rod I attach a green and chrome 4 inch Sling Blade dodger to the main line. To the rear of the dodger I connect a 36 inch fluorocarbon leader tipped with a shad pattern Hum Dinger. A lot of anglers attach their lures within a foot of the dodger, but Gary taught me to only do that with lures that have no built in action. For spoons and plugs that have their own action they don't require the added action they would get from being close to the dodger. In this case the only function of the dodger is to put out flash and vibrations, mimicking those created by feeding trout. Once I get the rod rigged, I apply some scent such as Pro-Cure Super Gel to the lure, free spool the lure and dodger back 100 feet behind the boat, attach it to the downrigger and send it down to 25 feet.

Once the downrigger is down and I put the rod in the downrigger's holder, I crank the reel until the rod is drawn into a deep bend. That way when a trout strikes and pulls the line out of the clip, the flexed rod will help get slack out of the line, reducing the chance that the trout will throw the hook. On my second rod I tie a swivel on the main line, connect a 36 inch piece of fluorocarbon to it and knot on a chrome and blue Cripplure. I free spool the scent smeared Cripplure out 200 feet knowing it will be working just below the surface and put the rod in a holder.

On your first rod you rig up with a watermelon colored 4 inch Sling Blade with a No. 2 black and white Needlefish spiked with shad scent trailing 3 feet behind it on a fluorocarbon leader. Once you finish rigging, you let the lure and dodger out 100 feet behind the boat, clip it to the downrigger and drop it to 15 feet. Next you rig your second rod with a fluorocarbon leader tipped with a Yo-Zuri minnow plug in the ghost minnow finish. After rubbing some herring scent to the lure, you free spool the minnow plug out about 200 feet behind the boat, allowing it to work about 6 feet below the surface.

With all the rods out we've got lures covering the top 25 feet of the water column. So at this point all we have to do is adjust our speed to 2 miles per hour, kick back and wait for a strike. Right? Well not exactly, trolling in a straight line will catch plenty of trout, but for maximum results it is a good idea to constantly turn and zig zag. This causes the lures to speed up and slow down as well as to rise and dip. A lure that displays this type of erratic movement will trigger more strikes than one that moves through the water at a steady pace and depth.

Now if we start getting hits, which is likely, based on what we observed with our eyes and the sonar, that's great. In that case all we'll need to do is determine which rigs, scents and depths are getting the most action and make changes so that all our rods begin drawing strikes. If we don't get strikes, what should be do?

I like to give my first spread of lures a decent chance to succeed, so I'll usually troll for about 30 minutes before I begin experimenting. The first thing you want to do is begin trying some different colored lures. If that fails to spark the trout it's time to break out Cripplures, Pro Secrets and perhaps an Apex Lure and begin slowing down until we score our first trout.

So there you have it, a basic overview of trolling strategy. If you take the information from this chapter and begin combining it with on the water experience, you'll be well on your way to boating trout consistently. So far we've only looked at the basics of trolling, of course there is a lot more to the sport than that. In the following chapters we'll explore many of the more advanced aspects of trout trolling.

Chapter Nine: Graduate Level Trolling

Whether I'm targeting bluegill in a farm pond or blue marlin off Puerto Vallarta I believe in keeping things simple and that goes for trout fishing too. An angler that makes use of the basic trolling approaches outlined in the previous chapter will catch trout in most situations all season long, yet there are a number of advanced tactics and tricks that can help elevate your success rate to a whole new level.

Let's begin by taking a closer look at downrigger tactics. In the previous chapter we discussed using a downrigger to troll single lines at a set depth. Many new trollers don't realize that more than one line can be trolled off a downrigger using a method known as "stacking"...as in stacking multiple lines on a single downrigger cable. On the other hand some veteran trollers are aware of the stacking approach, but don't incorporate it into their repertoire because they view it as complicated and fear tangled lines. With a little practice stacking can be a simple and efficient way to hook more trout.

There are a couple different approaches to stacking lines. One way is to use wire clips, known as stackers. These clips are teamed with releases and connected to the downrigger cable at various points as it is lowered into the water. Most anglers fish no more than two fishing lines off a single cable, but if you have multiple people on your boat it is possible to use three or more stackers on each downrigger, trolling a line off each of them. As a general rule the stackers should be placed no closer than 10 feet apart and the lines trolled off them should be no more than 25 feet long. Obviously, stacking is most useful when the trout are holding in deep water. In the extreme you could cover a 60 foot span of the water column by spreading out a total of six lines using two downriggers.

Now while you might think that fishing six lines is sure to result in tangles when a trout strikes that is usually not the case. You see when a trout grabs a lure, gets hooked and pulls the line from its release the fish tends to fall straight back initially because of the forward momentum of the boat. Provided you keep your lines short, a hooked trout will quickly swing out behind and above the other lines. The biggest drawback to using wire stackers is that they must be removed one at a time when you bring the downrigger up and attached one at a time on the way down. This can be a lot of work in situations where you need to raise and lower the downrigger often.

For anglers that won't be using more than two rods per downrigger there are some nifty devices on the market that make stacking a snap. The Shasta Tackle Company offers the Shuttle Hawk, while Sep's Pro Tackle markets the Simply

Trollin' Device. These devices are very similar to each other. They are basically small planer boards with a release attached to their rear edges.

The Shuttle Hawk works like this. You attach your first fishing line to a clip near the downrigger ball and send it down. You attach a small plastic stop to the cable 10 to 15 feet above the ball. Then you lower the first line down to the level you want to fish. Once the first line is down you slip your plastic planer to the cable, let out your second fishing line and attach it to the clip on the planer. The fishing line attached to the planer causes it to tip forward and dig into the current created by the movement of the boat. At that point all you need to do is loosen the drag on your rod all the way and the planer will be forced down to the plastic stop you put on the cable. Once it is all the way down, tighten the reel's drag and go about your business.

When a trout hits the lure trailing behind the planer and pulls the line out of the clip, the rolling weight in the planer moves to the rear, causing its nose to tilt upward. When it does, it catches the current and is forced back up to the surface. Many times I use my Shuttle Hawk even when I'm only using one rod per downrigger since it saves me from constantly raising and lowering my downrigger. I have electric downriggers, so I guess this makes me a little lazy. If you have crank downriggers these devices are real labor savers.

There is another method of probing different depths with only a single rod. I refer to this as using a cheater, it works like this. Let's say you're fishing a dodger and spoon 60 feet deep off a downrigger. A cheater or dropper is a 36 inch fluorocarbon leader with a spoon tied at one end and a snap swivel at the other. Once your downrigger has been lowered and the rod is in the holder, simply reach out and snap the spoon tipped leader to the line on the rod and drop it into the water. The pressure of the water pulling against the fishing line causes it to arch out behind the boat. The cheater leader will slide down the line to the center of the arch. If your primary rig is working at 60 feet the cheater will descend down to about the 30 foot level and stay there.

You can always count on the cheater stopping at the halfway point between the surface and the primary rig. Since the cheater is essentially only working from 6 to 10 feet behind the boat, depending on how large the bow in the main line is this tactic only works well when the primary rig is being pulled in moderately deep to deep water, otherwise the cheater will be too close to the boat for good results.

In general, for me to employ a cheater my primary rig has to be working in 40 feet of water or deeper. It is important to keep a close eye on your rod when using a cheater, since when a fish is hooked, it will almost never cause the line to pop off the downrigger. Instead you'll see the fight of the trout telegraphed to the rod. At this point you need to grab the rod, pop it out of the downrigger and quickly reel until you feel the weight of the trout. If you don't move fast the trout will often shake the hook because it is essentially fighting on a slack line.

While the cheater will often pick up trout as you troll it will also pick up the occasional bonus fish. Undoubtedly you've been reeling in a trout only to look down in the water and see another fish swimming along with it. In that situation the second trout hears the struggle of the hooked fish, assumes it is feeding and moves in hoping for an easy meal. At times when a fish is hooked on the primary rig and the line pulls out of the clip the cheater will slide down the line until it reaches the primary rig's dodger. If there is a second trout following the hooked fish it will often grab the cheater and you'll have a double header on your hands. Typically, you'll be fighting your fish and suddenly the fight will become sluggish and be replaced by heavy weight as the two hooked trout fight against both your rod and each other.

Most of the time small low drag spoons like Needlefish, Excels, Sep's Pro Secrets and Dick Nites are used on cheater leaders, but there are other options. Apex style lures work well as do Wiggle Hoochies.

If you are really daring you can employ both a lure and dodger on a cheater. I've seen it done and I've seen it catch fish, but all in all it seems like a lot of work. In reality if it takes a full blown dodger and lure combination to draw strikes you'll be best served shelving the cheater concept and just working your main line at the depth indicated.

Since we are talking about downriggers this is a great time to consider electrical currents as they pertain to repelling or attracting trout. A century ago researchers in Russia discovered that fish are highly sensitive to weak electrical currents. Positive charges of the correct intensity attract fish, while negative currents will cause them to shy away.

Dick Pool of the Pro-Troll Company is a pioneer in the science of electronic fish attraction. "Every boat takes on a natural electric charge in the water because of the different metals touching the water. The zincs on the motor will be positive in charge. This drives the bonded metal parts on the boat to a negative charge. Any unconnected metals like downrigger cables will take on a positive charge," relates Pool.

"Natural electrolysis causes electricity to flow from the metal hull parts of your boat to your downrigger cable. If the boat and downrigger are set up right, this will place a positive charge on the downrigger cable which attracts fish. A Black Box will stabilize this charge at the ideal voltage for the type of fish you are trying to catch," adds Pool.

"Modern downriggers offer fishermen a big advantage in getting the correct positive electrical charge around their boats. If the downrigger is insulated, natural electrolysis between the stainless steel downrigger cable and the metals of the boat will create a positive charge. The fisherman can then control and stabilize this charge to the ideal voltage by using a Black Box. Commercial salmon trollers have used the Black Box technique to increase their profits many thousands of dollars each year by imposing a voltage on their stainless steel lines. By using multiple cables all connected to the Black Box, they can create a complete zone of positive electricity around the boat's hull. Downrigger fishermen can create this same field with a Black Box," continues Pool.

So what is a Black Box? Without going into a highly detailed explanation, it is a device that can regulate a set amount of positive electrical current traveling along your downrigger cables. According to Pool, the Black Box is effective in improving results when trolling. It should be connected to all the downriggers on the boat, so it provides a uniform positive charge completely around the hull. This way there is a zone of fish attraction created at the downrigger cables, meaning fish will come to the cables. Often, results will be best when using a very short amount of line between the downrigger release and the lure or bait.

Furthermore Pool asserts that studies on trout have linked their response to electrical fields to their metabolism. Active fish such as trout have a higher rate of metabolism and demonstrate more electrical sensitivity. Research has shown that the best Black Box settings for most trout is . 65 volts. Mackinaw have also demonstrated the capability of sensing weak electrical fields in the water. The Black Box has proven very effective in attracting them. A setting of . 600 to . 650 is the recommended range for macks.

I look at technical electronic equipment like sonar units, GPS units and Black Boxes in much the same way as I do wrist watches. They are all great advancements that enhance my life. While I know how to use them to my best advantage, I only have a basic knowledge of how they work. In other words I'm not a technician! In college I earned degrees in Psychology and Education, while steering well clear of the Engineering Department. As a result I've just scratched the surface of Black Box technology and the science of electronic fish attraction.

Dick Pool and Joe Spurgeon have written a highly informative book on the subject titled, Black Box Technology. You can get a copy of their book by writing the Pro-Troll Company at P. O. Box 5788, Concord, Ca. 94524 or give them a call at (925) 825-8560. The book and a lot of other interesting information can be accessed on the Pro-Troll website at protroll.com. While my knowledge of the science behind the Black Box is limited, I can state with complete certainty that a Black Box is must have equipment for the serious troller. Employing a Black Box will enable you to catch more and larger trout, that's the bottom line!

At times when trout are holding in deep water the problem is getting your lures down to their level. Downriggers enable the angler to overcome this challenge. When the trout are holding near the surface another challenge arises. Many times if the water is clear, the surface is glassy or if the trout have been subjected to a good deal of fishing pressure the boat passing over them will spook the trout out to the sides and away from the lures. Most anglers including myself deal with this situation by pulling their lures from 150 to 300 feet behind the boat. This way when the fish flare they have a chance to calm down and drift back into the path of the boat before the lures arrive on the scene.

Side planers are a highly effective tool for presenting lures to fish holding near the surface without spooking them. While they are used extensively by anglers in the Midwest and east, most west coast anglers never give them a try. Almost every serious west coast trout troller you meet has downriggers, but I'd be surprised if one in ten of them had side planers. I've experimented with side planers enough to know that if we used them more we'd find ourselves putting more trout in the boat.

The uninitiated are probably asking, "What is a side planer and how does it work?" A side planer is a piece of wood, plastic or foam that when attached to a line, travels away from a moving boat based on its shape. These devices skim along the surface and track along from 50 to 100 feet beside the boat with 20 to 100 feet of line tipped with a lure or bait tailing out behind them. This enables the angler to present the lure to trout without moving through the area where the trout are holding with the boat.

There are a couple different types of side planers available to anglers these days. There are small inline models that are efficient, inexpensive and easy to use. Sep's Pro Fishing offers the Pro Side Planer. This inline planer can be adjusted to track either to the port or starboard. To employ this type of planer you let your offering out the desired distance behind the boat, attach the main line to the planer and then free spool the planer out the desired distance to the side of the boat. When a trout is hooked the planer partially disconnects allowing the fish to be fought with minimal resistance. Since these planers are small there are some limiting factors that have to be considered such as the size of the lure you are using, the diameter of the line, the amount of line behind the planer and wind will all reduce the distance from the boat that the planer can be pulled.

Anglers that become serious planer trollers will want to graduate up to the large mast pulled models that have become so popular on the great lakes. These planers require the angler to mount a short pole or "mast" in the boat. At the top of the mast there are a pair of large reels spooled with heavy line. These lines are attached to big stable planer boards that will buck stiff breezes and surface chop. On the rear of the planer there is a release just like the one you attach to your downrigger. After spooling a lure out the desired distance behind the boat the line is attached to the clip on the planer and it is spooled out from 50 to 200 feet to the side of the boat. When a trout strikes, the line releases from the planer.

This planer works exactly like a downrigger except that rather pulling the lure down into the water column it steers it out to the side. As is the case with downriggers, these large planers allow the angler to stack two or more fishing lines on the heavy line leading out to the planer. For example an angler could have three trolling lines working 50, 100 and 150 feet off both the port and starboard sides. As an extreme example if you've got enough anglers in the boat, stacking lines both off downriggers and planers will enable you to cover a substantial swath of water with a dozen different lures!

In addition to getting lures out of the path of the boat, planers can help anglers overcome another challenge that often arises during the fall at many lakes. In the fall when deep water reservoirs cool, the lakes' baitfish often move in tight to the shoreline and the trout follow them. Despite the fact that the trout are feeding heavily and will strike willingly, getting the lures close enough to the bank can be tough.

Gary Miralles targets these fish by maneuvering his boat out past points and then swings back toward the bank at a hard angle, causing his lures to sweep across the shallow water at the tip of the point. This works great for Gary because he intimately knows the contours of the lakes he fishes and has been practicing for 30 years. For the rest of us, using a planer offers a short cut to success. Simply let a lure out 30 to 40 feet behind a planer and then spool it out from 75 to 100 feet off the bank side of the boat. Once the planer and lure are out, it is a simple matter to steer them within feet of the bank while the boat stays in relatively deep water.

So far we've been talking primarily about presentation, before we move on to some advanced lure strategies and cutting edge attractors, I'm going to throw out a couple more thoughts about presentation. It would be helpful if you knew if trout were being attracted to your trolling spread wouldn't it? Well, there are a couple of ways you can do just that. The first way is to outfit your boat with Walker downriggers. Walker offers a camera that has an coaxial cable that doubles as a downrigger cable. By attaching this cable to a small television you can actually watch your rig working behind the downrigger weight.

Gary Miralles has one of these units and it is fascinating to watch. He has his teamed with a television that boasts an integrated VCR, so he can actually record what the camera picks up. When employing a camera you quickly learn that fish will often follow your lures for long distances without striking. Most of the time far more fish follow our lures than actually strike them. The camera allows the angler to constantly evaluated the attitude of the fish while experiment with lure color and action. This greatly speeds the process of figuring out what the fish want.

These cameras run about $1,000. Are they worth the money? Absolutely, if you've got the money to spend they will help you catch more trout because they help you quickly determine what the trout want, yet they are not essential equipment by any stretch of the imagination.

If you have a quality sonar unit you can usually determine if trout are being attracted to your spread when using downriggers. First of all as you troll, the downrigger weights should show up on the screen as a solid line at the depth you are trolling. As you pass over and through fish, watch their images. If they have a fine line or blur trailing away from them it indicates that they are moving. For example if your weight goes over a fish and a line is emanated from the bottom of the fish it indicates that the fish is moving up toward your gear. When you see fish moving into your spread and they are not hitting you can try to provoke a strike by shaking the rod. This sends small vibrations down to your rig and at times this is enough to spark a bite. You might also try dropping the downrigger down or moving it up a few feet. Sometimes this change in speed and direction will cause a reaction strike.

If you are not using downriggers, you should periodically drop your reel into free spool for a couple seconds. Gene St. Denis of Blue Ribbon Charters taught this trick to me. It causes a following trout to overrun the lure. Many times when you put the reel back into gear you'll be rewarded with a hooked trout. Another trick to employ when top lining is to quickly reel in a few yards of line. This makes a follower believe a meal is about to be lost and at times a violent strike will result. When pulling lures off of downriggers and side planers you can do the same thing by goosing the throttle once in a while causing the lures to accelerate forward.

Okay, enough is enough! Let's talk about lures. Trout are school fish by nature and this means that they are accustomed to competing against each other for prey. In the world of trout nothing fires up a large fish like seeing a smaller trout feeding in its vicinity. I don't know if this just excites the larger trout or if it actually believes the smaller fish is stealing it's dinner. In any event when a trout sees a smaller trout feeding the larger trout will often try to snatch the forage item away from its smaller buddy.

A few years ago a friend of mine told me about a rig he uses to tap into the competitive feeding habits of trout. To set the rig up you tie the main line from your rod to a three way swivel. To the remaining upper eye of the swivel you attach a six foot fluorocarbon leader tipped with a No. 13 rainbow pattern Rapala floating minnow. To the lower eye of the swivel you want to connect a five foot fluorocarbon leader with a small wobbling spoon such as a Hum Dinger, Pro Secret or Needlefish tied to it. When this rig is pulled through the water the minnow plug will dive and the spoon will run a foot or so in front of it giving the illusion of a small trout chasing a minnow. Most of the trout that hit will be hooked on the spoon, but at times they will nip at the tail of the minnow plug too. I don't use this rig very often, but it is something that has saved the day for me when nothing else was working.

There is another version of teaming a spoon with a plug that I stumbled on back in 1998. While out bass fishing I'd often have trout follow my rattling crankbaits right up to the boat. Every once in a while one of the trout would actually hit and get hooked, but in general my crankbaits were too large for them to grab. One day I was out trolling at a local lake. I'd fished all morning and I'd only picked up one trout. Looking through my tackle, I noticed a deep diving rattling crankbait and a thought struck me. What if I rigged a short leader on the back of the crankbait and tipped it with a small spoon? Thinking that the crankbait's rattles would draw the trout in and that they'd strike the spoon I wasted no time attaching the leader and free spooling the rig out behind the boat.

I'd been trolling no more than 10 minutes when a good size trout hit. I'd like to report that I landed the trout, but I never got the fish in. Instead, I abruptly lost the trout. When I reeled the crankbait in I noted that it only had about 2 inches of leader remaining on its rear. The leader had been cleanly cut and I figured that it had hung up on one of the crankbaits trebles and was cut by the barb. A few minutes later I had the hooks off the crankbait and another spoon tethered to it. The bite wasn't red hot, but the rig did help me catch four more rainbows, filling out my limit.

Ever since then I've employed the "crankbait rig" from time to time and it often results in hookup. I think it is something the trout just don't see and it arouses their curiosity. I don't like to use the rig off a downrigger. It is a good rig to use when the trout are holding in 10 to 20 feet of water, since depending on which crankbait you choose to use it will dive anywhere from 8 to 15 feet deep. For the rig to be successful it is critical to employ a crankbait that boasts internal rattles since it is the sound emitted that sparks the curiosity of the trout and draws them in for a closer look.

I'm going to conclude this chapter by talking about what many consider the most advanced fish attracting device ever invented. I'm talking about the Pro-Troll E-Chip. The E-Chip is a small electronic device that draws strikes from most predatory fish including trout. To understand how the E-Chip works it is important understand how gamefish feed. According to Dick Pool, the nervous system of every living organism puts off electrical current. Predatory fish can detected and pinpoint the voltage created by live bait. An E-Chip mimics this voltage and draws in predatory fish.

The E-Chip truly represents cutting edge technology. It does not require batteries. The E-Chip is a proprietary electronic crystal and ball incased in a stainless steel tube. In the water the crystal's hypersensitive electrons are activated by any movement or vibration. E-Chips have been independently tested by professionals that depend on catching fish for a living and they have confirmed the device's effectiveness. E-Chips make lures and dead natural baits seem alive to predators and this causes them to strike. In its first year on the market the E-Chip was used in less than one percent of fishing tournaments, yet it captured more than one million dollars in prize money for anglers in twelve countries that year. It is tough to ignore results like these.

Pro-Troll sells a line of lures, flashers and bait holders that incorporate E-Chips. In addition they also sell E-Chips separately that are mounted in a plastic sleeve that can be slid onto your line or attached to the lure or dodger of your choice. In my tackle box you'll find Pro-Trolls Electronic Trout Killers, these are Apex type lures that contain an E-Chip. I've also got a selection of loose on line E-Chips and some E-Chip equipped bait holders. We'll talk more about the bait holders a little later.

I get to exchange notes with a lot of professional anglers. Whether we are talking about trout, salmon, black bass or stripers, lures that utilize E-Chip technology often draw three times as many strikes as identical lures that don't make use of E-Chips.

Chapter Ten: Trolling With Natural Baits

Artificial lures have been around for a very long time, but it's a safe bet that history's first angler employed natural bait and that goes for history's first trout troller as well. These days with all the high tech gear and state of the art lures that are available to us, many trollers tend to overlook natural baits, despite the fact that they work as well today as they ever have.

At times when the going gets tough or when big trout are the objective some of the best trollers I know reach for natural baits in the form of frozen shad, anchovies or herring and live baits such as night crawlers and minnows. Monte Smith of Gold Country Sportfishing is a prime example of what I'm talking about. Monte is a highly talented guide that spends his time plying lakes such as New Melones Reservoir, Lake Don Pedro and Lake McClure in the California Mother Lode.

For big rainbows and browns as well as husky landlocked kings, Monte's number one offering is frozen shad. Here on the Pacific coast trolling or "rolling shad", as the technique is known among trout and salmon aficionados, closely mimics the way coastal saltwater anglers employ frozen anchovies and herring for tempting chinook and coho salmon. In fact in addition to shad, trouters often employ herring and anchovies too.

The term "rolling" stems from the fact that a properly rigged shad or anchovy will slowly roll through the water when trolled. Predatory fish like trout, are often in the presence of hundreds or even thousands of baitfish. Most of the time these baitfish are ignored because they are healthy and hard for the trout to run down. Yet, a slow moving baitfish that shows signs of distress is gobbled up in short order.

When a shad is rolled through the water it puts off vibrations consistent with those created by an injured baitfish. From a visual standpoint a rolling shad gives the impression of a disoriented shad minnow that has lost its ability to remain upright. Combining this with the vibrations a rolled shad creates and the fact that shad are the predominate forage in the majority of reservoirs, presents the trout with a series of cues that add up to trigger their feeding instinct.

"I soak the fresh shad I buy for trolling in brine overnight. Once I've brined them I divide them among several zip lock bags and freeze them. I add blue dye to some of the shad I brine. This way I can do some experimenting with color throughout the day as I troll," discloses Smith.

Soaking baitfish such as shad, anchovies and herring in brine firms and toughens them. Some anglers brine their bait by soaking it in a solution of two thirds water, one third ice and one or two cups of rock salt. I employ the same basic approach to brining, most of the time, but recently I've started using Pautzke Fire Brine. The results have been outstanding. Let me give you the lowdown on this new product and how I've been using it.

The thing I love about Fire Brine is the simplicity it offers. To brine bait with Fire Brine all you need is a bottle of Fire Brine, a 1 gallon Ziplock bag and some quality bait, be it herring, anchovies or shad.

Fire Brine is a liquid that comes in a 32 ounce plastic bottle. It is available in clear, blue, red, chartreuse, orange and purple. Fire Brine eliminates, multiple ingredients and mixing. Everything you need is right there in that bottle.

What's in the brine? I don't know and the guys at Pautzke aren't talking, but here's what I do know. Since 1934 they've probably cured about a billion salmon eggs so right there they've got an unmatched bait processing and preserving resume. When guys with a track record like that put their minds together and come up with a brining agent, you know there's a high probability that it's going to be the real deal!

Before I describe how to use Fire Brine, I should make the point that for top notch results you've got to start with top notch bait. Freshly dead bait that has been treated gently to preserve the scales is always best. Tray bait runs a close second and bag bait runs a distant third. The better your baits look going into the brine the better they'll look coming out and good looking baits almost always outfish so-so looking baits.

If your bait is fresh simply put it into a gallon Ziploc, shake your bottle of brine vigorously, pour in enough Fire Brine to cover the baits (a half bottle will take care of one package of tray bait) and place the bag in the refrigerator for 8 to 24 hours. After that you can remove the baits from the brine, put them in an airtight container and keep them cold.

I've kept the brined baits for up to 72 hours with no problems. If I'm keeping them longer than that, I'll freeze them. Bait brined and then frozen works just fine. You'll want to partially thaw them prior to rigging.

If your bait is frozen, run water over the bait for a few minutes so you can separate them without damaging the scales. Place the separated baits in your bag and cover them with brine. At that point seal the bag and let it set at room temperature for 6 to 8 hours, allowing the baits to completely thaw. Then place the bag in the refrigerator.

There was a time when I only trolled natural colored baits, but I've come to realize that baits died various colors can be deadly. I still rely on natural colored baits the majority of the time, but I use blue and chartreuse baits a lot too.

As near as I can tell when using Fire Brine, maximum color absorption is achieved after about 8 hours. While extending the stay in the brine beyond 8 hours doesn't result in bolder color it does result in tougher bait.

The color transferred to baitfish by Fire Brine is excellent. The entire bait takes on the color of the dye, but the natural flash of the baitfish is retained. The brines are also UV so you don't have to worry about applying UV gel or spray to your baits.

To make your brined baits even more attractive to the fish you can add scent to the brine. Krill scent is always a great choice for salmon fishing. If you want to add krill scent to your baitfish, simply get a bottle of Pautzke Fire Power krill powder and add about a table spoon full to your bag of baits and brine. Gently tumble the solution to ensure all the baits are exposed to the krill.

In addition to krill you might also consider adding a few drops of either garlic or anise oil to your batches of bait. Anise works great anywhere and everywhere and at times landlocked kings flock to the smell of garlic.

I'm not finished testing Fire Brine yet, but from what I've seen so far, Pautzke Fire Brine looks to be the simplest and one of the most effective approaches to brining bait.

Fire Brine toughens your bait and makes good bait better. If you choose to use colored Fire Brine to cure and dye your baits you can expect consistent rich color that does nothing to decrease the natural flash of the bait. Since Fire Brine is UV enhanced you can rest assured that the fish will see your bait no matter how deep you go.

Fire Brine is available at fine tackle shops throughout the West Coast. If your favorite tackle shop doesn't have it, tell them to order you a supply of Fire Brine from the folks at the Pautzke Bait Company.

Properly preparing shad and other baitfish is only part of the equation. The real challenge comes in rigging them so they display the proper rolling motion when drawn through the water. The Pro-Troll company offers a small shad size version of their renown EChip equipped rotary bait holder that has earned so much acclaim in the world of saltwater salmon trolling. The Roto Chip size No. 1 is a half inch wide and is appropriate for use with shad or other minnows that are from 2 to 2. 5 inches long.

For the uninitiated these plastic bait holders pinch on the head of the baitfish and sport a wing that makes them roll or rotate when trolled. The device is supplied on a leader sporting a pair of octopus hooks. The hooks are not hooked in to the shad, but rather trail alongside the bait as it rolls through the water. Roto Chip holders come in eleven different colors, three of which glow in the dark.

"Bait holders are simple to use and there is no doubt that they will catch fish. Overall I think the plastic head is too prominent. The whole point to using shad is to present the trout and salmon with a natural bait. I think this goal is defeated when you add a plastic holder to the head of the bait," Monte relates.

Monte ties a simple two hook monofilament leader that imparts rotation to the shad, while allowing them to maintain a natural appearance. The leader consists of a 36 inch section of 8 pound test fluorocarbon line tipped with a No. 8 or 10 red colored treble hook. Above the treble he slides on a small bead and then attaches a No. 8 or 10 red colored octopus hook on a sliding snell. To tie a sliding snell the first thing you must do is acquire a knot tying guide or go on the internet and find an illustration of how to snell a hook.

The sliding snell uses the same knot, the only difference being the piece of line the octopus hook is snelled on is separate from the leader. As the snell knot is tied the line is wrapped around the leader. When the knot is finished and trimmed you are left with the octopus hook attached to the leader in such a way that it can be slid up or down. If this sounds complicated, it is at first, but with a little practice it becomes pretty easy. I've seen some anglers simplify the process by using a pair of small rubber bobber stops to hold the octopus hook in place on the leader.

The octopus hook's ability to slide on the leader is very important since this is what ultimately makes the shad rotate. This is how it works. Select a shad and imbed one of the treble's points in its vent near the base of the tail. Next pin the octopus hook upward through the shad's nose. With the two hooks in the bait, slide the octopus down toward the shad's tail until a curve is created in its body. It is this curve that causes the bait to rotate. One of the nice things about using this type of leader is that it allows the angler to experiment with the intensity of the bait's spin. The straighter the curve in the bait the less it will roll, the sharper the curve the more violent the spin. You don't enjoy this type of versatility when employing a plastic bait holder.

In the past, one of the advantages to using a bait holder was that they come equipped with an EChip for added attraction. Now that Pro-Troll offers an inline EChip it is a simple matter to slide one on a hand tied leader and let it ride up against the shad's nose.

Monte is a big believer in using a Pro-Cure scent injecting bottle to inject scent oil into his shad and I am too. Herring, sardine, anchovy, krill, anise and predator scents are all great choices. I like to start out with baitfish scents before moving on to sweeter stuff like anise. The benefits to injecting scent are twofold. First of all the oil slowly leaches out of the bait and creates a scent trail. Not only does this scent trail lead trout to the bait, but it also encourages followers to commit and grab the bait. Beyond that, when a trout strikes at the bait, scent and taste are released encouraging the trout to gulp it in.

Over the years my thoughts on the best speeds for rolling bait have changed significantly. There was a time when I was convinced that the presentation had to be made slowly in the 1 mph range. The reason for this was twofold. First I thought that trout and other gamefish found a slow presentation most attractive when it came to trolling natural baitfish. Second I didn't think that a delicate shad or anchovy would hold up to the abuse of being trolled at anything over say 1. 5 mph.

The test of time has proven me wrong on both accounts. Trout and salmon will eagerly slam a quickly spinning baitfish and yes you can troll rigged bait up to and beyond 2 mph with little problem.

The brining process, particularly with a product like Fire Brine makes your bait tough and somewhat pliable. This means you can get it to conform to the shape you want and that the pressure of the current at even a fairly brisk trolling speed isn't strong enough to damage the bait or pull the hooks loose.

Of course your trolling speed has an influence on how much bend you'll want to put in your baits.

As a general guideline I like to run straighter baits for trout then I do for salmon. For salmon I like a big roll, but for trout I like a tighter more drill bit like spin. A big roll is best achieved at slow speeds, while a tight spin can be used at a variety of different trolling speeds.

Line twist can be a tremendous problem when rolling bait, but there are things you can do to eliminate it. The first most obvious solution is using one or more high quality trolling swivels between your leader and main line.

If you find yourself in a situation where you can only find the garden variety swivels Take a 14 inch section of heavy 25 to 40 pound test monofilament and put swivels at either end of it. Place this swivel adorned section of heavy line between the leader and main line. The thick mono will resist being rolled over by the lighter leader material.

Silver Horde markets a line of small trolling rudders. They come in chrome and other colors. These devices can be hard to find, but once you find them your tackle box should contain a selection of them. Rudders simplify rigging and make eliminating line twist easy.

The final element of consideration for an angler rolling bait comes in the form of the strike. Trout usually hit a trolled baitfish pretty hard. If you are using a downrigger a trout will usually pop the line out of the clip on the strike.

King salmon are found in a lot of trout lakes around the west and they strike rolled bait differently than trout, much of the time. A king salmon strike is usually signaled by a lot of tapping and nibbling. If this occurs when fishing with a downrigger, manually pop the rod out of the clip and then allow the forward motion of the boat to draw the slack out of the line. Generally as the boat moves away and the line starts to rise the hooks will sink home and you'll be eating barbequed salmon for dinner!

Shifting gears a bit, when exploring new lakes or targeting trout that are playing hard to get I have not found anything as effective as a threaded night crawler. To rig a threaded night crawler I start off by snelling a No. 6 bait holder hook on the end of a 36 inch 10 pound test fluorocarbon leader. Next I take out a night crawler and slide it onto my worm threader. If you've never seen a worm threader, it is a simple wooden handle with an 8 inch section of fine diameter metal tube imbedded in it. The tip of the tube is cut off on a sharp angle. Once I have the 'crawler impaled on the threader, I slide it down to the handle. After that I place the hook tip in the end of the tube and pull it down tight by gripping the leader against the wooden handle. The final step is to slide the 'crawler up the threader, over the bend of the hook and down the leader.

A night crawler threaded like this can be fished a number of different ways. You can tie the leader to a swivel knotted to the end of your main line and pull it from . 50 to 1. 5 miles per hour. Rigged like this the worm will spin and glide through the water, making an inviting target for trout. My all-time favorite approach is to pull a threaded 'crawler 12 to 18 inches behind a watermelon pattern Sep's Side Kick dodger or Strike Master dodger. The only time I go with a larger dodger is when the water is discolored or if I'm working in really deep water.

A threaded 'crawler pulled 18 inches behind a set of silver or brass flashers is an old school favorite that has been catching big numbers of trout for decades. Sep's makes fine low drag flashers for this work, but my all-time favorite flashers are the Vance's Little Slim Willie's. They are 17 inches long and feature three different blade sizes, simulating a larger fish "chasing" a couple smaller fish. These blades some in either chrome or chrome with prismatic chartreuse tape. I use both, but I use the chartreuse flashers the most.

I've noticed that when I have the flashers in the water, even if that rig isn't getting hit, my partner and I (often Paul Kneeland) get more hits overall provided we have our other lines working in the top 25 feet of the water column.

When targeting salmon in deepwater trollers often attach ball trolls to their downrigger weights to draw fish into their spread of lures and baits. Could it be that my near surface flashers are doing the same thing, namely pulling fish up toward the top and into a collision course with all the gear behind the boat, not just the lure trailing behind the blades?

Flashers definitely pull in and excite fish and when that happens the number of strikes you get should climb on ALL of your gear so long as it is running reasonably close to the blades.

I'm trying to be more observant and with this in mind I've gotten way more strategic about where I position the blades behind the boat. It seems to me that you want them working slightly in front of your other rigs. If our other rigs are running 75 to 100 feet back I'll often strip the flashers out 50 or 60 feet and fish them right off the middle of the stern.

As simple as 'crawler trolling seems there are a couple of tricks that can make using them even more deadly. These days I seldom use a night crawler without adding scent to it. At times I lube them up with Pro-Cure night crawler flavor Super Gel. At other times I'll inject them with oil or Pautzke Nectar. Believe it or not I've also found crawfish, krill, anise and garlic scents to be effective when teamed with 'crawlers.

When trout are spooky or finicky it is important to play out your bites, especially when using a plain threaded 'crawler or one teamed with just a small dodger. A trout that grabs a worm is not expecting to feel resistance. By playing out a bite, I'm referring to feeding the trout some slack when it hits. If the trout are being tentative a worm strike usually begins with a few taps. When I see that I immediately pop the line out of the downrigger clip and drop the reel into free spool, giving he trout a five or ten count before beginning to retrieve line. This allows the trout to eat the bait while feeling minimal resistance.

While there is a solid fraternity of trouters that routinely catch trout while still fishing or drifting live minnows, very few anglers use them for trolling. Those that do generally pin them through the lips on a single hook. When these intrepid anglers get a strike, a bare hook is typically all they have to show for their efforts. Trout seem to grab live minnows by the tail before turning them for head first swallowing. A trout that grabs a trolled minnow by the tail generally rips it off the hook and gets a free meal, while all the angler gets to experience is the agony of defeat.

I've found that trolling live minnows in the 1 to 2 inch range at 1 mile per hour or less produces good numbers of trout, provided the minnows are used on a double hook rig. I've caught rainbows up to 5 pounds while using the method I'm about to describe while fishing highly pressured reservoirs such as Folsom Lake in the Sacramento area.

My rig consists of a 36 inch 6 pound test fluorocarbon leader. For most applications I use an 8 pound test leader, but with live minnows I go light to give the minnow freedom of movement. On the end of the leader I tie on a No. 10 bronze octopus hook. About 2 inches up the leader I snell on a second No. 10 octopus. I pin the first hook upward through the minnow's lips. I don't impale the minnow with the rear hook. Instead I just let it hang loose so that it swings back and rides next to or just behind the minnow's tail when trolled. Nine times out of ten when a trout takes a nip at the minnow's tail the rear hook ends up imbedded in the cartilage at the tip of the trout's nose.

Since you'll be using a 6 pound test leader and the trout will generally be hooked lightly it is important to fish with a light drag. As is the case when rolling shad, I find that live minnows work best without being teamed with dodgers or flashers. The whole point to using live minnows is that you are making a subtle stealthy presentation. This goal will be defeated with the use of blades.

So are natural baits always the answer for trout trolling? While they will hook trout in most situations, they are not always the best choice. You are better off using artificial lures whenever possible, since they are easy to use and offer a high degree of versatility. However, when the odds stack up against you and most anglers are struggling to hook trout, don't hesitate to try pulling real meat. Naturals have kept me from getting skunked more times than I can count and they'll do the same for you.

Chapter Eleven: Hardcore Leadcore!

Everybody knows that leadcore stinks... It's heavy, it's lethargic and it's time has passed since anything you can do with leadcore you can now accomplish with a downrigger!

These are the assertions that a lot of trout and salmon trollers make in reference to leadcore line and I've got to confess, I've uttered a lot of these criticisms myself in the not too distant past. Yet from my current perspective I believe a lot of these assertions are off base, inaccurate or downright false.

Before I go any further let me make clear that I love downrigger fishing. All my boats in recent years have been fitted with a pair of Scotty electrics. My tournament partner Paul Kneeland outfits his Fish Sniffer Willie Boats with Cannon electrics...The point being that I spend a fair amount of time every year watching bent rods waiting for those "Oh So Sweet" releases. However there are times, particularly in the spring and fall when I never break out downrigger weights, because I can work just as effectively, perhaps even more effectively using leadcore. I'll tell you why....

The first thing I want you to do is picture that heavy old leadcore outfit your grandpa used. That's right it's that dusty tuna stick fitted with the sturgeon reel. Check it out, it's still rigged up with a five foot string of soda can size cow bells.... Now I want you to purge that image from your mind, because that's not the kind of gear I'm talking about when I talk modern Hardcore Leadcore fishing!

It was Monte Smith of Gold Country Sportfishing that first turned me on to modern leadcore trolling. Monte has become a high speed trolling guru over the past several years using his handmade Chucker T Spoons. Monte found that when working structure from a boat moving in the 3 mph range that lightweight responsive leadcore outfits were a lot easier to use than downriggers.

With the leadcore outfits everything is "direct drive" so to speak in that you don't have to play around with clipping lines to downriggers or mess with raising and lowering downrigger weights.

With leadcore all you need to do is spool the rig out X distance and you're fishing. Best of all, since a light responsive rod has replaced granddad's tuna stick, you won't be sacrificing much in terms of deadening the fight of the trout and salmon.

Initially I set my rigs up just like Monte set his up, but over time I've tweaked things a bit to meet my personal needs and I suggest you do the same. Here's what my rig looks like.

For a rod I employ 7'5" Vance's Tackle spiral wrapped E Glass trolling rod. As you'll see my rig makes use of braid, fluorocarbon and of course leadcore. All of these materials are low stretch and that's why I choose an E Glass rod over a graphite rod.

Vance's rods are highly parabolic and the action is slow. This cushions the strike and headshakes of the fish and keeps me from losing soft mouthed trout and kokanee.

The rod is matched with an Abu Garcia 6500 Line Counter reel. The reel is spooled with 200 yards of 20 pound braid, which is about the diameter of 4 pound mono. To the end of the braid I splice on 3 colors of leadcore. To the end of the leadcore I splice on 20 feet of 15 or 17 pound fluorocarbon tipped with a swivel. To the swivel I attach a 3 to 4 foot 8 or 10 pound fluorocarbon leader.

I played with several different knots for linking the braid and fluorocarbon to the leadcore, but the method I'm about to describe was not only the simplest, but also formed an extremely smooth connection that travels through the eyes of the rod without a hitch.

To make the connection, worm the woven sheath of the leadcore back and expose the lead wire inside. When you've got about 3 inches of the lead exposed, clip it off and then straighten out the now hollow sheath. Tie an overhand (granny) knot in the hollow sheath near the end of the lead wire, but don't draw the knot down tight.

Next slide the braid or fluorocarbon you want to connect the leadcore to into the hollow sheath and work it all the way up to overhand knot. Holding the braid or fluorocarbon in place inside the hollow sheath work the overhand knot down nearly to the end of the sheath. When the overhand knot is positioned about a quarter inch from the end of the sheath draw the knot down tight. That's it, you're done and you've formed a super smooth super secure connection.

With this rig I put on a lure or bait and run out all the leadcore. Then I spool the braid backing off and keep track of how much line I'm putting out using the line counter. Depending on how much backing I have out and the speed of the troll, I can reach down to depths of 25 feet or perhaps a bit more.

When using this rig not only can I adjust my depth quickly by simply letting out or retrieving line, I can also work the rod at critical times and give the rig some extra life and action. This comes into play when working shoreline structure while fast trolling spoons or Rapalas.

If I'm working fish holding deeper than about 30 feet I'll go with downriggers, but at times when the fish are from the surface to 30 feet deep I really like to use the leadcore.

Clearly simplicity is one of the corner stone attributes of modern leadcore trolling, but I believe it also offers anglers an added level of stealth. Let's face it downrigger weights and cables make a lot of disturbance when they come through the water. I'm convinced that sometimes this disturbance is good because it attracts fish. At other times I don't think it helps or hurts, yet I'm certain there are times when that disturbance puts fish off.

Leadcore allows you to reach moderate depths with a lot less disturbance you can with a downrigger. Leadcore isn't invasive. Its weight is distributed over its length, so it glides through the water very quietly with zero vibration.

So what sort of offerings do I pull off my leadcore outfits? Truth be told I pull all the same stuff I pull off downriggers. One day it might be a set of Lil Slim Willie Flashers trailing a worm for trout or an Uncle Larry's for kokanee. The next time out I might be rolling shad or pulling Apexs for trout and salmon at Shasta.

I rely heavily on my leadcore outfits during tournaments simply because they allow me to keep my baits in the water longer because I'm not messing with downriggers. Sure that may only come to a few extra minutes of actual trolling time over a two day event, BUT it may be during that extra few minutes that the kicker fish I need decides to strike!

In the last couple years I've been teaming my leadcore outfits with Sep's Side Planers at times with great success. I simply spool out all three colors of leadcore, attach the planer where the braid backing begins and then walk the rig off the side of the boat before putting the rod in one of the upper rocket launcher rod holders. This is a super stealthy way to go and I pretty much only troll this way with three different offerings, rigged shad, rigged worms or a Sep's fly teamed with an ActionDisc.

Beyond that there's not a lot more to know. Leadcore trolling is one of those core techniques that you should master. It's super simple to use, but it's also super deadly...Plus when that Abu's clicker screams as the rod bucks wildly in the holder, it's pretty darn exciting. A lot more exciting than a noodle rod popping out of a downrigger clip!

Chapter Twelve: Trolling From The Fast Lane

Fishing is like a lot of situations in life in that there are often multiple answers that are right and wrong and what's doing the job today, isn't necessarily going to fill the bill tomorrow.

As anglers we understand this rule thoroughly, yet at times we ignore it and fall into a rut as a result. No matter what type of fishing you think of, the best anglers are the ones that are able to use a broad range of approaches in order to adapt to the conditions at hand.

I think a lot of anglers that troll for trout and salmon in our inland lakes are locked in a "speed rut" and are catching fewer fish then they could if they'd just broaden their horizons a bit.

Over the years a lot of trollers have adopted the attitude that slower is better. Most trollers putter along between 1 and 2 mph and if kokanee are on the menu that range draws down even more to 1 to 1. 5.

Okay I recognize that there is a reason for this. When the fishing is tough, a super slow presentation is often the best option. I also understand that most trolling gear is designed to work best at these speeds. But what also needs to be recognized is that the fishing isn't always tough, sometimes the fish are active and chasing. And we can't lose sight of the fact that trout and salmon can swim upwards of 13 mph. They can and will run up and smack a lure moving at 4 mph without breaking a sweat.

Wait a second...do fish sweat? How would you know it's all wet down there? But you see where I'm going.

I'll concede that a nice slow troll is the correct answer at times, but at other times I'm convinced that you'll catch far more fish if you do your trolling from the fast lane. Let's learn how!

I typically start such discussions with a description of the tackle before moving onto terminal tackle and things like lures. Well, I'm switching gears in this case and we'll start off looking at some different lures.

It is true that most trout and salmon trolling gear is design for a slow to moderate speed presentation. When you start thinking about speeds from 2. 5 and up, your choices narrow quite a bit, but the lures that are available are highly effective.

One of the most effective and certainly the most famous fast trolling lure around is the Rapala. There's a long list of other minnow plugs that work great, but Rapalas are the most beloved of the bunch.

While minnow plugs are an obvious choice for fast trolling, many of us overlook a small array of spoons, both new and old that can make things happen on a fast troll.

The most famous and most readily available of these spoons is the venerable Speedy Shiner. Of course the name of this spoon alone is enough to tip you off that this is a high-speed offering.

"The "Speedy Shiner" style of lure appears to date back to the 1960's," says Peter Ridd of Thomas Lures, makers of the Speedy Shiner. "The lure probably originated in Maine. Back in those days a lot of companies were turning out spinning gear. It was customary then to offer a line of lures to go with your gear. The Speedy Shiner style lure was knocked off by a lot of different companies and there have been a lot of slightly different configurations of the spoon we market today. "

Lining up right behind the Speedy Shiner in terms of availability is the Hum Dinger. Not the little one, which is a fine trout spoon to be sure, but the big ½ ounce model that is constructed of thick heavy metal.

Rounding out the pack is a pair of lures designed by James Pagani. Pagani's lures can be hard to find in stores, but they can be found at his website www. sparklefish.com.

The centerpiece of Pagani's lineup is the Sparkle Fish. There is a smaller version of the Sparklefish dubbed the Golden Eye. These lures have a great reputation in the mother lode region, but they'll work anywhere a fast presentation is called for.

I think color is less important when trolling quickly then when moving slowly. If water clarity is anywhere near decent, I like to go with natural colored lures. That means chromes paired with hues of blue or purple for spoons. With minnow plugs, the same combos work well as does rainbow trout.

If the water clarity is poor, super bright stuff like florescent orange or firetiger can give you an edge.

When the light level is low either early or late or when the sky is overcast, black can be an absolutely deadly color that few anglers ever think to try.

When it's time to break the speed barrier dodgers and flashers are only going to slow you down. Most dodgers will begin spinning at around 2 mph, while with a few designs such as the Shasta Tackle Sling Blade you can push your upper limit speed up to about 3.

At times I'll use a Sling Blade, generally a 6 inch model when trolling quickly, but the vast majority of the time I run my lures alone.

I refer to anything over 2. 5 as fast trolling. When I decide that it's time for fast trolling that means I'll be working the 2. 5 to 5 mph range. Obviously fast trolling is an aggressive approach used to draw strikes from aggressive fish that are actively feeding.

A fast trolled lure will draw strikes out in open water, but it's when you work tight to structure that the method really shines. In reservoirs, trout, kings and bass orient to structure in the form of points and drops adjacent to deep water when feeding. They hold in these areas and ambush any baitfish that happen to swim within range, yet if anything threatens the gamefish they can simply melt into the depths.

When you show these fish that are fired up and in a mood to chase a fast moving lure, they only have a split second to react. Pounce now or let your dinner get away... BOOOOM ... FISH ON!

When the water is cold you can catch plenty of fish up near the surface while fast trolling toplined lures, but overall you'll be better served if you work a larger cross section of the depth range.

Naturally you can employ downriggers or traditional downrigger tackle when fast trolling. Since you'll often be working in tight to structure there is always the chance of a mishap (read that to mean snag) with your downrigger weight.

This being the case leadcore outfits make a lot of sense, but I'm not referring to that tuna stick your granddad used to use. I'm talking about a modern leadcore outfit intended for fast aggressive trolling.

Monte Smith of Gold Country Sportfishing is the one that first introduced me to "modern high speed" leadcore fishing. My rigs are a bit different than Monte's but the idea is the same.

For my rig I take a 7 foot Vance's Tackle rotator wrapped downrigger stick and pair the rod with an Abu Garcia level wind with a smooth drag, line counter and clicker. The rod is soft, but it is stouter than your typical kokanee rod.

I spool the reel with 200 yards of 20 pound braid which is about the diameter of 4 pound mono. To the end of the braid I splice on 3 colors of leadcore. To the end of the leadcore I splice on 20 feet of 15 or 17 pound fluorocarbon tipped with a swivel. To the swivel I attach a 3 to 4 foot 8 or 10 pound fluorocarbon leader.

With this rig I put on a lure and run out all the leadcore. Then I strip the braid backing off and keep track of how much line I'm putting out using the line counter. Depending on how much backing I have out, I can reach down to depths of 25 feet or perhaps a bit more.

The best thing about using a modern leadcore rig is the simplicity. You don't have to fool with downriggers or releases. Just put the lure in the water, strip off some line and you're fishing. When a fish is hooked you'll find the tackle to be light and responsive. And your heart will race when that clicker screams. Team a couple leadcore outfits with a couple toplined outfits and you and your partner will be able to cover a broad range of depths.

Chapter Thirteen: Fishing With Dodgers
(And We're Not Talking About Tommy Lasorda!)

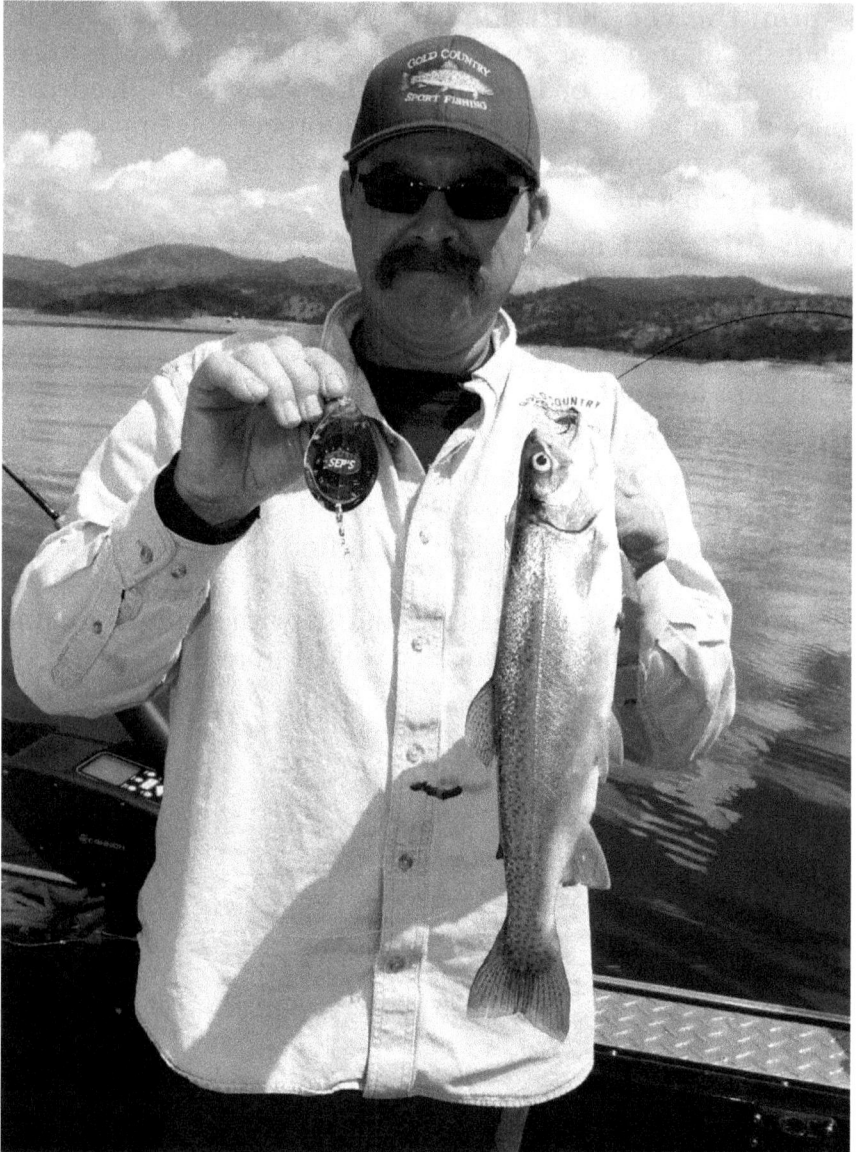

That's right I'm talking about those thin metal things you place on your fishing line not the Los Angeles Dodgers that everyone here in Norcal loves to hate and everyone in SoCal loves to love!

In looking through my personal archive of material from over the past 10 years or so, I find that I've never written a piece specifically about dodgers and I would venture to say this is true for many fishing writers. We all talk a great deal about lures and most of us are well aware of just how effective dodgers are at drawing strikes and putting fish in the boat, but apparently we aim to keep that information a secret since we don't write about them very much.

Well, as you've probably guessed I'm going to break the precedent in this chapter and I'm going to devote thousands of words to talking about dodgers and nothing but dodgers. It's going to be my dodger trolling manifesto!

Probably the first thing I should clear up for folks that are just getting into the freshwater trout and landlocked salmon trolling scene, is the difference between dodgers and flashers. At a glance dodgers and flashers look pretty much the same, but they perform very differently in the water. Dodgers wobble or kick side to side when trolled at the proper speed, while flashers spin a full 360 degrees. In freshwater, dodgers are used a whole lot more than flashers.

Here on the West Coast a lot of freshwater trollers refer to "lake trolls" as flashers, but they are not true flashers. Lake trolls are a series of rotating blades that work on a section of cable. Regardless of what you call them, lake trolls can help you box a bunch of trout, kokanee, kings and macks, but alas lake trolls are another subject for another chapter.

Back to dodgers. . . Dodgers basically do three things. They create vibration and flash. And they can impart an erratic surging motion to lures and baits, depending on how far you rig them behind the dodger.

It is thought that the vibration put off by dodgers is similar to those put off by feeding fish. Fish like trout and salmon have a strip of nerves along the lateral line that allow them to pick up and analyze vibrations in the water around them.

When the lateral line picks up vibrations that sound like fish feeding, predatory gamefish, being the opportunists they are home in on the sound hoping to pick up an easy meal. When they move in on the vibrations put out by a dodger and see your lure, they grab it.... That's the plan anyway!

While I think that vibration is the driving factor behind a dodger's ability to create strikes, you can't discount the fish attracting value of flash either.

For a long time I used to wonder just how much flash a dodger could possibly produce. One early morning not that long ago, I was heading out to meet my fishing partner hours before dawn for a day of kokanee trolling. I had several pre-rigged rods leaning in the front passengers seat of my truck.

As I approached an intersection where there were a handful of cars moving in different directions there was a sudden bright flash that I swear illuminated the entire cab of the truck. My eyes were adjusted to the dark and it was almost as if a flash bulb had gone off. Looking around I realized that the beam of another vehicle's headlights had hit the chrome surface of a 4-inch dodger attached to one of the rods. That incident left no doubt in my mind as to the ability of even a small dodger to create flash significant enough to draw fish in from many yards away. Conversely in the wrong situation they can also throw off enough flash to scare fish too, but we'll get into that a little later.

Dodgers come in a variety of styles and sizes. "Herring Dodgers" are oval shaped on either end, have an upswept edge at either end and a uniform width. A lot of companies market a line of herring style dodgers. Familiar names include Vance's Tackle, Sep's Pro Fishing, Luhr Jensen, Worden's Lures, Mack's Lures, Dick Nite and Gold Star. Some of these models are made out of thicker metal than others. This of course makes them heavier and they run deeper than thinner lighter models.

Another popular style of dodger is the thin or tapered dodger. The Shasta Tackle Sling Blade sets the standard in this type of dodger. Sling Blades are larger at the rear than they are at the front and they have a constant taper throughout their length. These dodgers only have an upswept edge at the rear end.

You should be aware of a third type of dodger that a lot of folks refer to as mini dodgers. Popular examples of these dodgers include the Sep's Side Kick and Sep's Strike Master along with the Crystal Basin Wild Thing. These dodgers are basically teardrop shape and cupped at the rear end. The Side

Kick is 2 inches long while both the Strike Master and the Wild Thing are 3 inches long.

Herring dodgers can typically be found in 4, 5, 6 and 8 inch sizes, while Sling Blades come in 4, 6 and 8-inch version. I've caught both salmon and trout while running big 8-inch dodgers, but in most situations you'll be best served with dodgers in the 4, 5 and 6-inch class. Having said that you should have all three types of dodgers I've described including mini dodgers in your tackle assortment to cover all the variables you are likely to encounter out on the water.

When fishing for trout and kokanee I start out with 4-inch dodgers and they usually do the trick. Once in a while I'll break out a 6-inch dodger when targeting these species. I think that larger dodgers can give you an edge when working deep water. I also use 6-inch dodgers when targeting late season kokanee. Late season 'kokes like lures with lots of action and 6 inch dodgers impart aggressive movement to kokanee size lures.

For king salmon, I've had the best results when running 6-inch dodgers. I attribute this to the fact that kings are usually found in large expanses of open water and as a rule hold deeper than both trout and kokanee. In wide-open deep water a larger dodger puts out more vibration and flash and seems to pull fish from longer distances.

Now that we've gone over the basic styles of dodgers available, it's time to think about dodger color.

Dodger color is confusing to a lot of anglers. Dodgers come in about as many color schemes as lures. Common questions include, what colors are best? How many different colors do I need? And do I need to match lure color with dodger color?

The first question is a sucker's bet. There is no best color, as it's the light level, water depth and water clarity that dictate the best color for a given day.

As to how many colors you need, the simple answer is that collecting dodgers gets addictive and you'll surely end up with a lot more color schemes than you actually need! Dodgers are something you don't lose too often, so it's pretty easy to end up with 50 or more of them after a few years of just buying one here and there.

Finally as far as matching lure color to dodger color goes, some guys I know are very careful about doing this while others pay no attention to it at all. I'm in the no attention at all camp.

While I've got a bunch of dodgers and certainly catch my share of trout and salmon, I'm no expert. This being the case, I picked up the phone and called up a pair of the most knowledgeable guys I know when it comes to trout and salmon gear and put the color question to them.

My first call was to Vance Staplin of Vance's Tackle Company. He's been manufacturing dodgers and guiding for many years, so his observations carry a good deal of weight.

"Color means a lot, but it's really the conditions that dictate dodger color," Vance related. "Early in the day when light level is low, you want flash. So chrome is a good choice as are glow models. When the light level increases you'll typically benefit from toning down on flash. When the sun is high and the water is clear the intense flashing of a chrome dodger can actually scare fish away. You can tone down your spread by swapping your chrome dodgers for copper, brass and painted models. "

"Everyone has colors and color combinations that they have a lot of confidence in. You want to keep an open mind. Make logical color choices, but really let the fish tell you what they want. Having said that, there are colors that really work well for a given species. For example, when I'm targeting rainbows I almost always have something green or chartreuse in the water, simple because that color has proven itself for me so many times," added Vance.

My next call was to Gary Miralles of the Shasta Tackle Company. Gary like Vance is a tackle manufacturer with a ton of experience and he too is a well-respected guide. Gary's line of Sling Blade dodgers are well known and have put a bunch of big fish in the box over the years including the current world record kokanee.

"For me more than anything else dodger color is about depth and the light level," Gary related. "When I pick out a dodger I think about the depths I'm fishing and the color spectrum. Colors disappear as you descend in the water column. Up top your reds and oranges show up well. In the middle depths greens work well for me and when I really drop

110

down deep where light penetration is minimized I like blues, glows and of course UV. When I'm fishing for trout up near the surface during stormy weather or anytime the light level is really low, I tend to lean toward darker colored dodgers. I think a darker color creates a more distinct silhouette for trout looking up toward the surface. "

Depth, light level, water clarity, light penetration and on and on. You can think and rethink everything when it comes to fishing and one fact remains constant, fish love to break the rules and seem to get a kick out of driving us anglers crazy! With that in mind I'm going to toss out a few colors that I've found to be very consistent producers a lot of the time.

I've had great luck running chrome and green, chrome and blue and watermelon colored dodgers for trout, particularly rainbows. To my knowledge I don't think I've encountered a situation where rainbows are put off by excessive flash.

When it comes to kokanee I've done very well with chrome and green, watermelon, bright orange, pink and glow models. Kokanee can absolutely be put off by too much flash. For 'kokes I start off bright early and then as the day goes on switch over to coppers. I've caught lots of kokanee on pink, watermelon and UV Sling Blades, chrome/green and copper/pink Vance's Dodgers and Sep's dodgers in glow/orange stripe and watermelon.

For kings I've had good luck with chromes, pinks, UV and glows. Kings seem to like plain Jane chrome dodgers just as much as they do the wild looking stuff. When it comes to crazy colors and kings, I've had a good deal of luck with the Sep's UV fruit salad color.

One last thing I should touch on before turning my attention to rigs is trolling speed. When you are trolling with dodgers you want to be moving fast enough to cause the dodger to dance back and forth, but not so fast as to make the dodger flip over and spin. Of course the best way to determine the best speed for a given dodger is to put it in the water right beside the boat and match the boat speed to the best action of the dodger.

Herring style dodgers offer aggressive action at low speeds. As a general rule most small herring dodgers will start spinning at around 1. 8 miles per hour. On the other hand slim

111

Sling Blade style dodgers don't offer real aggressive action at low speed. They typically perform best from 1. 8 to 2. 5 or even 3 miles per hour.

Mini dodger behave much like herring dodgers in that slow is the way to go. Much more speed than 1. 8 or 2 and they start to roll.

Okay some dodgers work better fast while others perform well at slow speeds. There are a couple tricks you can employ to make Sling Blade style dodgers work better at low speeds and to keep herring style dodgers from spinning when trolled faster than 1. 8.

If you take a Sling Blade out of the package and put it in the water at 1. 5 mph it will have a pretty subtle back and forth wobble. To make it really kick at this sluggish speed, take the blade in your hands with the face side up. Pushing upward with your thumbs work your way up and down the blade and bend a slight arch into it. The more arch you bend into the blade the more action it will have. Use careful measured pressure and test the dodger to see how the action of the blade changes. When it comes time to use the blade for fast trolling again, you can simply bend it back to its original shape.

Split shot is the remedy for a herring dodger that rolls when trolled too fast. While observing a blade working beside the boat figure out the speed where it wants to spin. Pull the blade out of the water and place a split shot on the leader immediately behind the snap on the rear of the dodger. The additional weigh will help to tame the rear of the dodger and in will maintain its kicking motion rather than rolling. The more weight you add the faster you can go to a point. You won't extend the speed range a great deal, but you should be able to break the 2 mph barrier.

When you find yourself out on the water and it's time to rig up, there are only two types of lures to choose from, lures with built in action like spoons, spinners and plugs and lures that produce no action of their own like hoochies, flies and kokanee bugs.

Lures with no action need to be rigged closed enough to the dodger such that the dodger imparts a surging dart ahead motion to them. As a basic rule you want to position these types of lures two to three dodger lengths behind the blade. If you are using a 4-inch dodger and fishing a kokanee bug behind it, the bug should be on a leader that is 8 to 12 inches long.

Lures that have action give you more latitude. Some guys say that you want spoons and spinners 4 to 5 dodger lengths behind the blade, but other guys use much longer leaders than that. When targeting trout with Hum Dingers and Cripplures trolled behind Sling Blades Gary Miralles often runs leaders in the 30 to 36 inch range and catches plenty of fish.

The type of lures you are using plays a part in the type of leader material you use. With lures that have action 8-pound test fluorocarbon is about right. 8 pound has enough strength to deal with big strong trout, but it is flexible enough to allow lures to work well.

When using lures without action you want to use heavier stiffer leader line in the 10 to 12 pound range, because stiffer line will transmit more of the action from the dodger to the lure. As a general rule remember that it's trout that can be leader shy. Kings and kokanee tend not to be. A lot of the successful tournament kokanee guys I know run 10 and 12-pound line on their gear.

In closing I'll toss out one particular rig that will put a bunch of trout in the boat for you over the course of a year. I knew about this combination for a long time, but it was Monte Smith of Gold Country Guide Service that really illustrated to me how effective it can be.

Monte spends a lot of time fishing at Don Pedro. Don Pedro is home to kings, kokanee and trout. Most of the time when Monte takes you out on Pedro the focus is on catching salmon. Monte typically rolls shad deep for kings and runs a couple lines armed with kokanee lures shallower.

This approach covers you for kings and 'kokes, but hanging out above the kokanee, often not far beneath the surface, are the rainbows. Too hook them Monte rigs up a threaded night crawler and trolls it 18 inches to two feet behind a mini dodger. When I first met Monte his dodger of choice for this work was a Sep's Side Kick, but these days he uses the new Sep's Strike Master quite a bit.

When the going gets tough for trout no matter where you're fishing break out the mini dodgers and worms. This combination will often catch trout when nothing else will.

Chapter Fourteen: Flasher Trolling Today!

Flashers or more correctly, "lake trolls" have been a cornerstone tool of trout and landlocked salmon trollers for at least a century. When all else fails you can slow troll a fly or threaded worm behind a set of flashy, jangling, rotating blades and you'll likely hook up...This tactic worked for our great granddads way back when and it still works today.

The nice thing about employing flashers today is that we have access to state of the art blades that are light and produce minimal drag while putting out a maximum amount of flash and vibration.

As a kid, I remember seeing the "Cow Bells" and "Ford Fenders" that Sierra Nevada trouters employed back in the 70's. The blades were huge and the cables they were rigged on were stout. As a result the tackle used for pulling this hardware had to be stout too. These guys always caught trout, but with all those big blades and the cue stick type rods you wonder how much the fight of even a 2 or 3 pound rainbow would be felt?

Say what you will about "the good old days", those '70's era trollers would have been overcome with joy if they had access to the high performance, lightweight, low drag flasher options that we enjoy today...Let's explore how these blades can help you catch more trout and landlocked salmon.

Like dodgers, flashers are attractors. Their job is to attract trout and salmon close enough to see your trolled lure or bait. They accomplish this task by putting out vibration and flash. My personal theory is that these predators mistake the vibration and flash of flashers for those put off by a small school of shad or other baitfish. On the other had I believe they perceive a dodger to be another gamefish feeding.

Today's average troller is obsessed with dodgers. I'd bet at any given foothill lake on any given day the number of dodgers being trolled outnumbers the number of flashers in the water by a ratio of 15 or 20: 1.

Often times perception trumps performance and this is doubly true in the world of fishing tackle. Anglers want the latest and greatest. At times they will walk away from tried and true offerings in favor of something sexy and new, despite the fact that the tried and true stuff was still producing fish with consistency.

This seems to be what happened with flashers. The flashers of today are undoubtedly the most user friendly and effective ever invented, yet far fewer anglers are using them today then were using lake trolls 40 years ago.

That's okay though... Let the dodger boys keep on doing what they're doing. Less guys pulling flashers only means that our flashers will produce more fish, since flashers aren't something the trout and salmon see as often as dodgers.

So far I've rolled out a pretty big wind up for a subject that is really pretty short and simple, because trolling with flashers is one of the simplest yet most effective approaches you can take.

With a long list of different companies turning out dodgers, it would be natural to assume that the market is flooded with flashers, but that's not the case. The three primary sources of flashers that I utilize are Vance's Tackle, Sep's Pro Fishing and Luhr Jensen.

Vance's offers both "Slim Willie" and "Lil Slim Willie Flashers". The Lil Slim Willies (LSWs) have always been plenty large for me, so I've never bought a set of the larger Slim Willie blades.

I spend a lot of time every season dragging my willow leaf LSWs for trout and kokanee. They work great for top lining early in the season and later on I run them first off leadcore and then off a downrigger if necessary. When toplined on 100 feet of 10 lb. mono at standard trout speeds LSWs run about 10 feet deep.

The LSW is unique from other flashers because the larger blade is at the rear. This resembles a striking fish feeding on smaller minnows. Even though the rear blade looks pretty large, drag is minimal. I often topline these on a Vance's Tackle downrigger rod without overloading the rod.

LSWs come in nickel, nickel silver fish scale, red fish scale, chartreuse fish scale and blue fish scale. All of them work well, but chartreuse is my absolute favorite color for rainbows!

Sep Hendrickson has forgotten more about trout and salmon fishing than most of us will ever know and that's why his line of Pro Flashers have always sported models with either Colorado or willow leaf blades.

If given a choice Sep's willow leaf blades are the way to go because they offer very little drag. Most days the willow leafs work just fine, but at times when the water is dark or muddy or when the fish are holding deep, more vibration in the form

117

thumping Colorado blades is just what you'll need to generate strikes. Sure the Colorado blades generate more drag, but if they dredge up strikes when other offerings fail, I'll make the sacrifice!

Sep's Pro Flashers come in a variety of different colors including silver/chartreuse, gold/red, black/chartreuse, copper/red and watermelon.

The use of these different metals creates flashers that put off a variable amount of flash. The most flash is thrown by the silver models, followed by gold, and then copper puts off the least.

Luhr Jensen is not only a huge tackle manufacturer, but they are the folks that kicked out a lot of those famous blades of yesteryear like Cow Bells and Ford Fenders. If you'd like to sample a little retro trout trolling all those great products are still available at the Luhr Jensen website at www. rapala.com. (Luhr Jensen recently became part of the Rapala family).

On the website you'll also note that Luhr Jensen also offers a full line of different state of the art ultra-light models aimed at kokanee and trout trollers. These Colorado and willow leaf blades come in chrome or brass or combinations of the two. An array of different accent colors are available.

Okay, you know flashers work and you know where to get them, but how do you use them? This is where things get really simple. To catch fish all you need to do is attach the blades to your line, add a short 14 to 24 inch leader to the back of the blades, attach an offering to the leader and start catching fish...That's it!

For trout slim profiles spoons work great. Needlefish and Excels are good, but I really like the little guys like Sep's Pro Secrets, Dick Nites and Sockeye Slammers.

Trout also respond really well to grubs and trolling flies worked behind flashers and of course the number one trout trolling offering of all time is a threaded worm rotating lazily behind those sexy spinning blades!

If my life depended on catching a trout while trolling, I'd go with flashers and a worm...That's saying a lot, there are a bunch of different lures in my tackle box!

When kokanee are the target I generally rig an Uncle Larry's spinner behind my blades, but at times you'll find me pulling a small spoon too. Usually an orange or pink Dick Nite or Sockeye Slammer.

Back in the old days color choices were pretty much limited to chrome or brass and the old timers caught plenty of fish. This being the case you might be wondering if we need all the colors we find on the market today? Probably not, but at times having that perfect color will help you catch an extra fish or two.

Over time you'll develop your own favorites, but if you are out to buy your first ever set of flashers get two pairs, one in chrome and one in brass. When you want a lot of flash go with the chrome blades when you want to be a bit more subtle go with the brass.

Chrome works great for kokanee early in the day, as the sun gets higher sometimes the chrome bite will die, but if you put out a set of brass blades you'll start getting strikes once again. This is because when the sun started hitting those highly reflective chrome blades it started scaring the salmon away rather than drawing them close.

For rainbows, too much flash never seems to be an issue. As a result when I'm trout fishing I usually run chrome blades all the time. As I said earlier I really like the combination of chrome and chartreuse for rainbows. Are they better than straight chrome blades? I don't know for sure, but I do know I fish the chartreuse ones with more confidence and that's an important part of success.

Over the course of a year I catch a lot of fish using flashers. In doing so I've noticed something else that is worth mentioning even though it is circumstantial evidence at best...

I've noticed that when I have the flashers in the water, even if that rig isn't getting hit, my partner and I (often Paul Kneeland) get more hits overall provided we have our other lines working in the top 25 feet of the water column.

When targeting salmon in deepwater trollers often attach ball trolls to their downrigger weights to draw fish into their spread of lures and baits. Could it be that my near surface flashers are doing the same thing, namely pulling fish up toward the top and into a collision course with all the gear behind the boat, not just the lure trailing behind the blades? Flashers definitely pull in and excite fish and when that happens the number of strikes you get should climb on ALL of your gear so long as it is running reasonably close to the blades.

I'm trying to be more observant and with this in mind I've gotten way more strategic about where I position the blades behind the boat. It seems to me that you want them working slightly in front of your other rigs. If our other rigs are running 75 to 100 feet back I'll often strip the flashers out 50 or 60 feet and fish them right off the middle of the stern.

Chapter Fifteen: Big Spoons...Too Big For Trout, Too Small For Salmon?

Like most anglers, I spend a lot of time thinking fishing. Why did I get skunked that day? Why did they bite this day? Would the number of strikes I get go up if I ran brighter lures? You get the idea!

One subject that has been on my mind a lot in recent years is spoons, or more specifically trolling spoons and that's what we'll be talking about in this chapter.

When it comes to spoons both freshwater anglers that chase trout and saltwater anglers that work the ocean for kings seem to be stuck in a bit of a rut.

Trout trollers rely heavily on spoons, but almost all the time we are pulling spoons that range from small to absolutely tiny. We don't hesitate one second to tie on a big plug like a Rapala or a Trophy Stick and we are more than happy to pull a full size 4 inch long night crawler behind a set of blades, but show us a spoon much over 2 inches long and we'll tell you it's way too big for trout.

Ocean salmon guys operate pretty much the same way only in reverse. When we are out on the salt looking for kings we are thinking big fish. Sure a 26 inch keeper is dandy, but a 26 ponder is what we are really hoping for!

This being the case, most saltwater salmon guys are obsessed with big baits like 4-inch anchovies, 6 to 8 inch herring, 4 to 6 inch hoochies and chunky spoons ranging up to 7 inches. These anglers aren't interested in running anything small because they assume that a small offering decreases their chance of getting that magnum size fish.

In fishing, often times, the beliefs of anglers and the reality of what actually happens out on the water are two distinctly different things and that is certainly the case in the scenarios outlined above.

If the trout are on the bite and you want a shot at a larger than average grade of fish, break out those big baits INCLUDING large spoons in the 3 inch class.

Big spoons for trout, small spoons for saltwater salmon...There are a lot of spoons available that fill this description such as large Needlefish, Shasta Tackle's ½ ounce Hum Dingers, Kastmasters, Speedy Shiners and Krocodiles. All the spoons I just mentioned and more will get the job done for both trout and salmon. Not long ago I stumbled on a line of spoons from the folks at Silver Horde that seem especially well suited to playing the dual role of big trout spoon and small salmon spoon. The spoon is called the Kingfisher Lite.

The KingFisher Lite, or KFL comes in 3 different sizes. The No. 3 measures 5/8" x 2 5/8", the No. 3. 5 is 7/8" wide and 3" long, while the No. 4 is 7/8" x 3 3/8". I don't have any No. 3 spoons, but I have a bunch of 3. 5s and 4s.

KFLs do an exceptional job of imitating a wounded baitfish. The folks at Silver Horde have been turning out topnotch fishing gear for over 50 years, so they know how to design an effective spoon. The special shape built into the KFL gives it a really seductive swimming motion. If it's a disoriented wounded look you are going for slow your troll down. If you want to give the impression of a panicked fleeing baitfish, speed things up.

The spoons are made of brass and are very light in weight, hence the name. The light weight of the spoons, makes them very responsive, so they work well when teamed with either medium or large size dodgers.

For me shape and action are the two most important cues when it comes to generating strikes, but color plays a factor too. I give the KFL two thumbs up in terms of silhouette and action. The fact that the KFL lineup includes a long list of both utilitarian and creative finishes is only icing on the cake.

I'll level with you...I'm the editor of the biggest fishing magazine on the West Coast. The folks at Silver Horde sent me all the colors in the lineup but you don't need to follow that route. What you need is a well thought out color selection and you need at least two lures in each color you choose. Why two?

You need two because these are great spoons and at some point you are going to break them out when strikes are hard to come by and they are going to turn the day around for you...and if you only have one you know what will happen.... Snap! Your moment in the sun is over if you don't have a replacement. Just saying....

You'll find standard, double glow and UV finishes in the KFL lineup. The colors I use most for trout and landlocked kings are the same colors I use most for ocean kings. Here are my favorites in descending order. Silver Horde doesn't name the finishes of these spoons only identifying the finishes by number: No. 731, this is a UV watermelon finish. No. 650 UV Chrome. No. 651 UV Chrome w/purple stripe and No. 652 UV

Chrome w/green stripe. No. 675 UV Double Glow cop car and No. 677 UV bloody cop car.

Every once in a while I'll tie on a super bright model like No. 616 wonder bread or No. 624 a Double Glow green, white, pink and orange monstrosity that nothing should hit, but everything from bass to salmon grab it anyway.

Your favorite tackle shop likely has a supply of KingFisher Lite spoons, but if not tell them to order some for you from the folks at Silver Horde.

Silver Horde/Gold Star has an awesome website that details all of their fine products including KFL spoons. You can check them out at www. silverhorde.com.

Chapter Sixteen: The Deadly Apex

What is the perfect trolling lure for trout and landlocked salmon? Or better yet what are the characteristics of the most consistently productive trolling lures for trout and landlocked salmon?

In reality no one can answer this question definitively, but most of us have an opinion. I've spent thousands of hours trolling for trout and salmon over the course of my fishing career and I've had the privilege of fishing with some of the best guides and anglers on the West Coast.

Based on what I've seen the best lures offer vibration, erratic, unpredictable or "skip beat" action and a baitfish like silhouette. It is also important that the lure has the ability to be trolled quickly. In generally a fast presentation not only draws more strikes overall, but a fast moving lure also accounts for a lot of larger than average size fish.

This makes sense since the fast delivery allows you to cover more water, expose the lure to more fish and draw strikes from the most aggressive fish. I believe that a fast moving lure tricks large experienced fish into striking because they never really get a good look at the lure. The lure zooms in and they have a split second to either strike or let the opportunity pass...

So what lure offers all of these properties? Well there are several, but based on the title of this piece you've probably already guessed that my top choice is the Apex Trolling Lure...Well you're correct!

The Apex meets all the criteria I've outlined and it's also a lure the angler can experiment with to produce action that is absolutely unique...Let's dig deeper!

Apex Lures are manufactured by the HotShot Company. HotShot is a top manufacturer of ocean salmon fishing gear and the original generation of Apex Lures were designed for ocean kings. These large Apex Lures ranging up to 6 ¼ inches remain a favorite of ocean salmon trollers from California to Alaska and throughout the Great Lakes.

With large Apex Lures slaying ocean salmon, it's not surprising that a member of the HotShot brain trust came up with the idea of offering smaller Apex Lures designed for trout and landlocked salmon. The end result of this thinking is the Apex Trout Killer Series and the Apex Kokanee Special Series.

Master kokanee angler Phil Johnson helped the folks at Hot Spot develop the Kokanee Special. The lure employs two red chemically sharpened Gamakatsu octopus hooks that are snelled from ¼ to ½ inch apart. When these super sharp hooks are combined with the unique Apex rigging that allows the Apex blade/body to slide up its leader leverage is taken away from the kokanee. When a kokanee is hooked on a traditional spoon, it can shake it's head against the weight of the lure and get the hook loose.

This doesn't happen with the Kokanee Special. The harder the kokanee shakes it's head the further the lure body slides up the leader. Kokanee Specials come in 1 and 1½ inch sizes and are offered in several different standard and UV color schemes.

The Apex Trout Killer also comes in 1 and 1½ inch sizes and is offered in a bunch of different color patterns. The hooking arrangement is different on the Trout Killer. Instead of double hooks the trout version has a single J-hook attached via a swivel and the hook eye also sports a small willow leaf "kicker" blade.

Truth be told, I've caught trout on Kokanee Specials and I've caught kokanee and kings on Trout Specials. Over time I've concluded that the hooking arrangement on the Kokanee Special is better overall then the set up on the Trout Killer, so in the end all of my trout and kokanee Apex Lures end up rigged the same way with a one basic differences.

When kokanee are the target I go with a pair of either Gamakatsu or Eagle Claw Lazer Sharp No. 8 octopus hooks. I use red hooks if I have them, but black nickel works just as well for me.

When I'm looking for trout or kings I employ a No. 6 octopus nearest the lure and put a No. 8 hook behind it. When I'm trolling Apex Lures for trout and kings I'm really targeting fish in the 3 pound class or larger. When I'm successful in drawing strikes from these larger fish, knowing that a No. 6 hook is embedded in the jaw of the battler gives me confidence!

You'll note that between the hooks and the body of the lure, the Kokanee Special sports a pair of glow beads. These beads might seem like a trivial detail, but they are an important strike triggering factor when trolling for 'kokes during periods of low light or in deep water.

These beads are also important because they create space between the hooks and lure body. When I re-rig any of my Apex Lures whether for trout or kokanee I employ the kokanee style beads. Sometimes I use glow beads, sometimes UV beads and at other times simple plastic prismatic beads that I get at the craft store.

Leader size and tipping are a couple issues we should focus on for a moment. Some guys get a new Apex and run in right out of the package and don't re-rig until the leader gets frayed. Other guys re-rig right away. I'm in the re-rig right away club. For kokanee I like a 10 pound test fluorocarbon leader. When I'm aiming for trout and kings I go with 12 pound fluorocarbon. Again when I'm pulling Apex Lures, I'm thinking big fish and I want a leader that is up to the challenge.

When I refer to tipping I'm referring to tipping the lures hooks with strike triggering bait. For kokanee shoe peg corn or Pautzke Fire Corn is the way to go. All you want is a single kernel on the rear hook.

For trout I rarely tip at all, but if I do, I'll use a tiny bit of worm. For kings you'll benefit by tipping the rear hook of your Apex with a tiny sliver of anchovy fillet that has been cured in Pautzke Fire Brine.

The main thing to remember when tipping is that you want to check the action of the lure beside the boat. If your piece of corn or bait is too bit the action of the lure will be impacted.

And what about lure color? For most light conditions or depths Kokanee Specials in Hot Pink, Flame Orange or Kokanee Red produce well. These finishes have high fluorescence on their backs for bright light conditions, while the bellies are glow in the dark for low light conditions or deep water fishing.

For bright days when the fish are in the top 15 feet of the water column the Flame Sparkle finish is good since it has high fluorescence on both sides with added sparkle.

When the day is overcast and the fish are holding in water that is 60 feet deep or less Chartreuse or Chrome FishScale are proven producers.

For trout and kings I like to stick with standard baitfish colors to start with and then I'll go brighter if the fish don't respond. If I had to run only one color Apex I'm tempted to say it would be watermelon, because that finish is so deadly on trout, kings and 'kokes, but a few years ago I stumbled on a pattern that is even more effective...It's the clear/UV finish from the Kokanee Special lineup. It's a clear piece of plastic! I have no idea why the fish respond to it so well, but they do. Trout, kings, coho, kokanee, spotted bass...everything loves my clear Apex!

Now we come to trolling speed. I stressed earlier that I like a fast presentation. Of course presentation speed is relative to the type of fish I'm targeting. For kokanee I prefer to run my Apex Lures from 1. 8 to about 2. 2. For kokanee that pretty fast and I've actually hooked a good many kokanee trolling Apex Lures much faster while fishing for trout. For trout and kings I ramp things up even more running from 2 to 2. 8 mph or even faster.

Generally these brisk trolling speeds work out just fine, but if I think I need to slow down, Apex Lures will still perform well at lower speeds. The only thing you might need to do is lighten the leader since the heavier leader material tends to deaden the action when trolling at slower speeds.

Early in this piece I talked about experimenting with Apex Lures to create unique action. Unfortunately I'm out of space so we'll have to cover "Apex Modification" for another article. For now though I'll leave you with this thought...When you look at an Apex you'll notice that the leader is threaded through some small holes in the lure's body. Using your own drill armed with a tiny bit, you can make your own holes and your lures will have a totally unique action...

Finally, if I don't address it I know I'll get emails.... Do I use dodgers or flashers with Apex Lures?

Rarely, some guys do and catch plenty of fish, but when I'm pulling Apex Lures or rolling shad for big fish I like to go with a really stealthy natural presentation so I leave the blades in the tackle box.

Chapter Seventeen: The Hoochie Revolution

Have you ever noticed that the simplest lures and presentations are often the best? Lures that are painstakingly created to exactly match the forage gamefish feed on are often, indeed almost always, upstaged by simple impressionistic offerings.

In terms of simplistic lures there are few that are simpler than the hoochie. For folks that aren't familiar with them, hoochies are nothing more than hollow plastic "squid", basically a plastic skirt that can be slipped on a leader, rear hook of a lure or even on a jig head.

Hoochies in the 4 to 6 inch range first stormed onto the West Coast fishing scene as lures used for ocean salmon trolling. Commercial salmon anglers in particular embraced hoochies because they found them nearly as effective as anchovies and herring, but much simpler and faster to rig than baitfish.

These days hoochies remain an important tool for ocean salmon anglers, but relatively recently anglers that target trout, kings, kokanee and coho salmon residing in lakes, discovered how deadly small hoochies in the 1. 5 to 2 inch size range can be.

If you are a trout or landlocked salmon angler that has yet to try trolling with hoochies, it's time for you to get started. Not only will hoochies help you catch more fish, but they also help you save money since they are significantly cheaper than a lot of other offerings.

I would say that one of the things that really appeals to me about hoochies beyond the fact that they catch fish and don't cost an arm and a leg is the versatility they offer. There are a bunch of different ways to rig them depending on whether you are fishing them alone or teaming them with another lure or natural bait. Fished alone they closely match the shape and action of a small baitfish.

Teamed with baits and lures they add a dimension that few fish have seen and when you show fish something they haven't seen your chances of getting hit rise dramatically. Let's take a look at some of these rigging options and how you can use hoochies to the best advantage.

For starters there are three kinds of hoochies you'll find on the market. These include loose unrigged hoochies, rigged hoochies and wiggle hoochies.

Wiggle hoochies come pre-rigged with a long leader and a pair of hooks and are fitted with a special clear plastic lip that make them wiggle pretty much the way a crankbait does.

Rigged hoochies come out of the package rigged with a fairly long leader and a pair of hooks. Some companies offer plain pre-rigged hoochies, while other companies offer hoochies that are downright fancy with added tinsel and flashabou.

As you probably are guessing I use all three types, but most often develop my own rigs using loose unrigged hoochies. For basic trout, king or kokanee fishing I rig a hoochie like this. I take a piece of 12 pound fluorocarbon leader material that is about 20 inches long and snell a pair of No. 6 or 8 octopus hooks on the end of it, such that they are from 1 to 1. 25 inches apart and facing in different directions.

Next I slide on a pair of 1/8 inch glow in the dark beads. With the beads in place I slide a hoochie on the leader with the skirted end facing toward the hooks. I slide the hoochie down to the beads and hooks and work the beads inside the hoochie's body.

Hoochies, with the exception of wiggle hoochie, have no built in action. So whether you are using a hoochie you've rigged yourself or one that came out of a packager pre-rigged, you'll have to use a dodger to give the lures some action.

As a general rule you'll want the hoochie to be 2. 5 to 3 dodger lengths behind the rear of the blade. If you are using a 4 inch dodger that means you'll want your hoochie from 10 to 12 inches back. Rigged this way the dodger will give the hoochie a very seductive pulsing speed up and slow down motion.

When I'm rigging hoochies for targeting king salmon and kokanee sometimes I want a little extra attraction such as when the fish are holding in deep water so I'll team my hoochies with E-Chips. I accomplish this by sliding an E-Chip on my leader instead of the beads. I smear a little BioEdge fish scent on the E-Chip to act as lubricant and then push it into the body of the hoochie. As the hoochie dips and darts behind the dodger the E-Chip puts out a steady stream of fish attracting electric pulses.

When I'm fishing for kokanee I naturally tip my hooks with corn. When coho or kings are on the menu I like to tip my hooks with little pieces of anchovy, herring or shad. I think the taste of real meat really encourages the salmon to get the lure well back into their mouths, resulting in better hookups and more fish landed.

I spend a lot of time rolling baitfish and pulling threaded worms when I'm trolling and I regularly use hoochies to enhance both of these presentations. The next time you rig a shad or anchovy for rolling or thread a worm slide a hoochie down the leader after the bait is rigged. You want the hoochie draped over the end of the bait.

Teaming hoochies with natural baits is a real winner, but few freshwater anglers are doing it. Saltwater anglers have long known how effective this tactic is for species as diverse as salmon, halibut and even marlin.

Hoochies are a natural choice for spicing up spoons and crankbaits. With spoons simply slip a hoochie over the back hook. You'll need to use a fairly large spoon so that the hoochie doesn't ruin the action, but when you get the right combination the look is very seductive.

To apply a hoochie to the rear of a crankbait you'll need to work a little harder. Using a slit ring pliers remove the rear treble from the bait, slip a hoochie over the hook and then put the hook back on the bait. If you do this I guarantee that your Rapalas will stand apart from the Rapalas being pulled by everyone else you know.

Let's move on to the wiggle hoochie. The wiggle hoochie looks goofy and honestly I avoided using them for a long time, but I've got to admit that they are a deadly trout lure. I've caught dozens of hefty rainbows on them and I've watched Fish Sniffer Publisher Paul Kneeland catch dozens more.

We run our wiggle hoochies without the addition of dodgers and they work great. At time I'll put wiggle hoochies on a 36 inch leader and slide them down a deep downrigger line as a dropper. While fishing for kokanee at Don Pedro, I had to stop using my wiggle hoochie dropper because I was catching so many rainbows that I wasn't able to keep my kokanee lure in the strike zone for any length of time.

What about hoochie color? For trout and kokanee I usually go with bright pink or orange hoochies. For kings and coho I start out with baitfish colors. Hoochies are so economical and come in such a diverse range of colors, it doesn't make sense not to have a wide range of colors represented in you tackle collection. Sometimes the fish want natural colors and at other times those crazy bright combination colors are deadly. Don't forget a selection of UV and glow models too...

Chapter Eighteen: Using The Wigglefin

A few years ago I filmed a striper trolling DVD with legendary Delta striper skipper Barry Canevaro. The overriding theme of Barry's instruction is that action catches stripers.

The same line of thought can be applied to trout, kokanee and landlocked king salmon. Action and vibration catch fish and as trout and salmon anglers we know this or we wouldn't have tackle boxes full of various dodgers and flashers.

While it's true that action and vibration do create strikes, showing fish the same presentation time after time, conditions them to that presentation and the chances that they'll strike are significantly reduced. This is especially true of big experienced fish that aren't actively feeding. Show these fish something they've seen time and again and they'll have no problem laying off of it. Show them something new that looks to be an easy meal and even though they aren't feeding they'll often take a swipe at your offering.

Am I advocating for you to get rid of all your tried and true dodgers and flashers, because trout and salmon that have survived a season in almost any or our reservoirs have seen everything in your tackle box multiple times? Yes I am and you can send them to me at the Fish Sniffer office.

I'm being silly, of course I'm not advising you to stop using your standard trolling hardware. What I'm advocating is for you to add a unique and innovative device to your arsenal that will add "chaotic action" to your trout and salmon offerings that is far different than the action created by standard dodgers.

Some of you have heard of Wigglefin ActionDisks, but I'll bet that most of you haven't. As you can see from the accompanying photos ActionDiscs are funnel shaped plastic disks that slide on your line in front of lures and natural baits.

ActionDisks take advantage of the principle of chaos to generate a very realistic non-rhythmic swimming action and vibration. The movement is realistic and non-mechanical. It presents the fish with movements and vibrations they are unfamiliar with and hookups are the result.

So how do you use ActionDiscs? From my experience they are best teamed with offerings such as soft plastics, hoochie, flies, brined baitfish and worms that have no action of their own.

ActionDiscs come in two sizes. Series 1 ActionDiscs are the smaller of the two sizes and are best used with baits that are less than three inches long. Series 2 discs are larger, so they'll provide movement for larger heavier offerings. If you are targeting trout and landlocked salmon with standard sizes offerings you'll want Series 1 discs. If big browns, mackinaw and perhaps ocean salmon are on the menu Series 2 discs work well with larger baits and lures.

ActionDiscs come in clear, pink, chartreuse and orange. I want the fish focusing on the lure or bait, not the disc, so I tend to go with clear most of the time. But when the water is stained and visibility is low, brightly colored discs certainly have their place.

In addition to the discs themselves you'll also want some of Wigglefin's SideLock Stoppers. These are self-gripping stoppers that you feed your line through that allow you to instantly and precisely position the ActionDisc in front of your offering. This allows you to alter the action of your rig until you determine exactly what the fish want.

I've played around with ActionDiscs a good deal over the past few years, so I'll share some of the rigs and combinations I've found to be effective. Before I do that, I want to make clear that while most anglers use ActionDiscs while trolling they work just as well for bank anglers and boaters that employ a cast and retrieve approach. Any of the rigs I'm about to describe can be used for casting and retrieving, you simply have to add an appropriately heavy bullet weigh in front of the disc for casting weight and to get the rig down into the water column.

When fish are holding near the surface, trollers can also make use of the bullet weight method to fish offerings just under the surface without employing downriggers.

The first time I ever used an ActionDisc I was trolling up at Eagle Lake and I teamed a small disc with an orange Sep's trolling fly and within 20 minutes I'd boated a pair husky rainbows with a combined with of just over 7 pounds! And those trout came on a day when the full moon was making for very tough fishing.

The season after I caught those trout on flies, trolling plastic grubs stormed onto the scene at Eagle, pushing trolling flies out of the spotlight. Most guys troll grubs by themselves relying on the action of the tail to produce strikes, but I can tell you from experience on days when the business on plain grubs is slow, adding an ActionDisc in front of your grubs can change your luck quickly!

I've always enjoyed trolling threaded 'crawlers for trout. At times I team them with flashers, but more often than not I prefer to fish them naked, rigged to slowly roll when drawn through the water. When I started teaming 'crawlers with ActionDiscs I was blown away by the action. If you put the disc near the head of the worm the action is wild and all over the place. If you put some space between the worm and the disc using a stopper the action becomes much more fluid and seductive.

I'm running out of space so let's turn our attention to salmon. Hoochies, Kok-A-Nuts and Matrix Paddletails are my favorite artificials to use for landlocked kings. I've caught a bunch of fish while pulling these lures behind dodgers, but when I want to give the salmon a new look I've done well while teaming them with ActionDiscs.

With hoochies and Kok-A-Nuts I like to create some space between the lure and the disc. When using a Matrix Paddletail I like to thread a treble hook tipped leader through the bait so that the treble rests just under the bait's tail. I then slide on a disk and push the neck that protrudes from the disk into the head of the bait. What you end up with is a soft baitfish imitation that looks like a shad or smelt that's had its tail dipped in turpentine!

If you really want to go into stealth mode when targeting kings, provided you are fishing a lake that allows the use of baitfish, get yourself some live shiners that run two to three inches long. Put ice and rock salt in a cooler and then add just enough water to make the mixture slushy. Drop the minnows into the slush and they will die instantly and become firm.

Using a threader impale a shiner on a treble hook tipped leader with the hook protruding from the minnow's vent and the leader exiting out its mouth. Slide a stop on the leader and position it two inches in front of the bait and then slide on a small disc. Troll the rig from 1. 5 to 2 mph at the level the kings are holding and be ready, because it usually doesn't take long to get hit!

You can use the same approached with brined shad, small anchovies or an anchovy fillet pinned on a two hook leader.

For kokanee fishing you can team ActionDiscs with all your standard kokanee spoons and spinners, but where they really shine is when you team them with hoochies and bugs. Simply use a stop to position the disc the desired distance in front of the offering and go to work.

Want to try something few 'koke anglers are using? Snell a small red octopus hook at the end of a leader. Put a stop two or three inches above the hook and thread on an ActionDisc. Bait the hook with a couple pieces of corn or a tiny salad shrimp or a half shrimp teamed with a single corn kernel. Using this method the bait is the bug...Hmmm, are the gears of your mind turning?

If you'd like to get your hands on some ActionDiscs for the upcoming trout and salmon season or to view Wigglefin's full line of products including trolling flies check them out on the web at www. wigglefin.com. The website also has some great video of ActionDisc enhanced baits in action!

Chapter Nineteen: Bait Fishing For Boaters

The day before a foot of fresh snow had fallen. Overnight the cloud cover had broken up and the air temperature plummeted. When Gene Rush and I woke up about an hour before sunrise the temperature was hovering in the teens. At the cabin the air was crystal clear, revealing an impressive array of shimmering stars dotting the sky from horizon to horizon.

Launching my Gregor a short while after dawn we encountered a wall of dense fog hanging over the lake's surface. While the lake's temperature was a chilly 39 degrees the difference between water temperature and the frigid air was great enough to prompt the formation of fog.

With the low light level and little fishing pressure, trolling seemed an obvious choice until the water temperature was factored in.

Anytime the water temperature drops below the middle 40's trolling for rainbows becomes a sketchy proposition. They will still feed readily at these temperatures, but they won't move very far or very quickly to do so.

This is why I advised Gene that we stood a much better chance of hooking trout if we anchored up and fished bait rather than trolling. Gene was agreeable, so we slowly motored out of the marina and I set a course, using my hand held GPS unit, for a series of rocky shelves in an area that boasted several underwater springs.

It was an area that featured well oxygenated water, shallow feeding areas and instant access to the security of deep water. The two mile run to the spot took us over a half hour, since the fog forced us to move along at little more than idle speed. But, as soon as we started cruising over the shelves the sonar unit started registering multiple fish and I knew our patience was going to pay off.

After dropping the anchor on the shallow side of the shelves in 20 feet of water, Gene and I each rigged our spinning rods with slip bobber set ups and baited our hooks with lively baby night crawlers. After pitching the rigs out we put the rods in their holders with the reels open. Gene's bobber was adjusted to fish his worm 10 feet below the surface, while I had mine set for 15 feet.

Our baits had been in the water for a very short time when Gene's bobber started to twitch and wiggle before slowly disappearing into the dark water. Knowing that the trout would spend a good deal of time mouthing the worm, I cautioned Gene not to set the hook too quickly. Finally after about 30 seconds of waiting, line started to steadily stream out of Gene's spinning reel. Closing the reel's bail Gene allowed the line to tighten and drove the hook home.

At first the trout showed little reaction and Gene was able to quickly reel it to within a few yards of the boat before it woke up and started making fast hard charging runs. The fish was strong and determined, but it was no match for the unrelenting pressure of the spinning rod. We'd been fishing for less than 15 minutes when Gene slid the first trout of the day, a fine 3. 25 pound rainbow, into the net.

Over the course of the next three hours, Gene and I were in trout fishing heaven as we battled rainbow after rainbow in the 2 to 4 pound range. That night while eating dinner at a lakeside restaurant we overheard a bunch of local guides that had spent the day trolling, talking about how tough the fishing had been. That made our success all the more gratifying.

It's a sad fact that when many anglers make the transition from bank fishing to fishing from a boat they get caught up in what I like to call the "trolling rut". These anglers, perhaps on an unconscious level have the belief that because they have a boat they must troll whether they are catching fish or not. Don't get me wrong, trolling is a great way to catch trout, but it doesn't work all the time. There are plenty of instances when trout are sluggish or inactive and just won't chase a moving lure. At such times if you really want to catch trout your best bet for success is soaking natural bait.

Bait fishing from a boat is a simple yet highly effective proposition. Unlike the bank angler that most often fishes floating baits off the bottom, the boat angler uses a couple different techniques to suspend baits at various levels below the surface.

The simplest method of all is to either anchor up or drift with a bait hanging directly below the boat. A light spinning rod spooled with 6 or 8 pound monofilament is well suited for this work. To rig up begin by tying a small swivel to the end of the line. Tie a 24 inch 6 pound fluorocarbon leader to the swivel and tip it with an appropriate hook. Above the swivel add a split shot or two to get the rig down.

A variety of different baits can be effectively fished in this manner including worms, salmon eggs, cured roe, crickets, mealworms, small anchovy fillets or live minnows. The only baits that should be avoided when using this approach are floating baits like PowerBait, Pautzke Fire Bait, Power Eggs and marshmallows. Since the line will be hanging down directly below the boat in most cases, a bait that floats up will sit next to the main line and tangles will inevitably result.

All things considered, my favorite baits for fishing from a boat are baby night crawlers or minnows. These baits are alive and provide a lot of subtle movement that really makes them attractive to tentative trout. Since the trout that are generally targeted while bait fishing from a boat are inactive, applying scent to baits can mean the difference between success and failure. My favorite scents include anise, anchovy, herring, predator and garlic.

This method of fishing is especially popular at lakes that feature a lot of natural forage in the form of both aquatic insects and minnows such as Lake Almanor near Chester, California.

In lakes that have a massive abundance of food, the period when trout are actively feeding and willing to chase lures is short and the trout are seldom hungry. Instead of seeking out actively feeding trout, anglers zero in on the areas were the trout hang out between active feeding periods. While the trout might not be focused on foraging, they still have a hard time passing up a vulnerable slow moving offering presented right in front of them.

At Almanor anglers suspend baits just above the bottom in areas that feature springs to catch a variety of handsome rainbows, browns and landlocked king salmon. Overall, this method works best for targeting trout holding in close proximity of the bottom, but it will take suspended fish in open water too. In open water situations, you've got to rely on your sonar unit to pinpoint the depth of the fish and then you must strip line off the reel in one or two foot increments until you know your bait is hanging just above the level of the fish.

An interesting kink on this method that anglers at Almanor employ, is working a small crappie style tube jig in either a pearl or smoke color just off the bottom. The jig is either baited with a small strip of anchovy meat or heavily coated with anchovy scent. While fishing from an anchored boat the jig is lowered to the bottom and then reeled up about a foot. With the lure hanging in the strike zone the angler holds the rod and shakes the rod tip ever so slightly, imparting a quivering motion to the bait.

When you first begin using this method I have to admit that it feels pretty silly, but when the rod loads up and you find yourself locked in battle with a husky rainbow or brown, you'll quickly become a believer!

Free lining is an alternative method for suspending your bait below the boat. In free lining the same rig used for suspending baits is used, except no weight is added. The hook is baited, most often with a worm, and the rig is cast as far as possible from an anchored or slowly drifting boat. When the bait hits the water simply engage the reel and set the rod down. The bait will slowly filter down through the water column. When the bait sinks down to the bottom or comes to a rest directly below the boat, it's time to reel it in slowly and make another cast. The advantage of employing this method stems from the fact that the presentation is very natural and allows you to hit a variety of depths with each cast. As deadly as the simple presentations I've outlined so far can be, my preferred method of fishing bait from a boat is just a bit more sophisticated.

I like to employ slip bobbers because they give me the versatility to hit a variety of different depths, while systematically probing structure with slowly moving baits from an anchored boat.

Earlier we explored how to rig up for slip bobber fishing, so I won't review those points here. Instead let's consider how the boat angler can employ slip bobbers to the best advantage. Here in California we have the option of buying a second stamp for our fishing license that allows us to use a second rod in inland waters. This is an invaluable tool for all trout anglers, but it gives a special advantage to bait anglers. I find it to be a real boon when employing slip bobbers.

When trout are spotted on a sonar unit, seldom will they be holding steadfastly at any one depth. Instead they will be spread across a depth range, let's say 10 to 30 feet for an example. Slip bobbers give a pair of anglers armed with second rod stamps the ability to easily probe this entire depth zone by spreading out their baits at 10, 15, 25 and 30 feet. When the trout start biting it is often possible to refine the depths fished based on which baits are getting hit most consistently.

Now, when exploring these depths my partner and I don't set in the boat passively. Instead, we are constantly working. The first thing I do when selecting a spot to fish is determine the direction the breeze is blowing. Even if there is not a breeze things typically drift in a given direction.

Once I figure out where I think the trout are holding and which direction the drift will be, I anchor the boat up wind or up drift, of the trout. With the anchor set we both cast our first lines off the rear quarter of the boat, my partner fishing from one side and me working the other. Our second rods are tossed out off the front quarter of the boat. The rods are set down in the boat with the bails on our reels open, so line can flow out freely.

We allow our rear bobbers to drift back as far are 200 feet behind the boat, before reeling them back in and casting them out of the boat's front quarter. In this way our baits are constantly on the move and being rotated. When a bobber goes under it is typically best to let the fish run a short distance before engaging the reel and retrieving any slack that exists between you and the fish. Once the fish is felt, a short jabbing hook set is all that is needed to result in a solidly hooked trout.

This method is among the stealthiest for working points, offshore humps, reefs, ledges and expansive flats. I'll never forget the 5 pound rainbow I caught using this approach while fishing at Eagle Lake outside of Susanville, California.

It was late November and the lake's weeds were dying quickly. With so much dead vegetation drifting around, trolling was pretty frustrating, since I spent most of my time picking weeds off the lures. While cruising around in the lake's northern basin I located a 12 foot deep trough cutting across a flat that ranged from 6 to 8 feet deep. It seemed to me that rainbows traveling across the flat would use the trough as a corridor, because the extra depth would give them a feeling of added security.

Well, to make a long story shorter, after checking the wind I determined that the wind was blowing in roughly the same direction that the trough ran. This meant that if I anchored up on the edge of it, I could pretty much drift my worms right down the slot. By the time I set the anchor and had my lines in the water there was only about an hour of daylight left and I was a long run from the launch ramp. At most I'd have 30 minutes to fish. The spot seemed so good that I expected action to come quickly, but the fish, if they were there just didn't want to cooperate. With my fishing time nearly exhausted, I went about organizing my gear before reeling in my lines.

The breeze was up and there was a pretty good chop on the water, so when I looked up and couldn't immediately locate one of the bobbers the last thing I thought of was the possibility that a trout had taken it down. Scanning the water for several seconds I finally caught a movement out of the corner of my eye. Turning to the left I spotted the bobber cutting through the chop as it moved into the wind. Grabbing the rod I started working the reel. As soon as the slack was picked up the rod pulsed into a deep bend and line started streaking off the spool against the tension of the drag.

The trout was powerful and determined not to come near the boat. At times the trout would come to the surface and I could see a big clod of weeds on the line that certainly weren't helping my cause. My strategy was to keep the rod high, using its flexibility to put pressure on the hefty 'bow. After a 5 minute fight that seemed like 30 I was able to guide the trout to the boat and into my net. If it wasn't for slip bobbers there is no way I would have caught that handsome battler, that's for sure!

Chapter Twenty: Trolling For Trophy Brown Trout

I'll never forget the day I caught my first big German brown. It was the week after Christmas and since I was working as a school teacher I had the week off work. I knew there were anglers that specialized in catching hefty browns by speed trolling with minnow plugs. There is a reservoir, named Rollins Lake situated about 15 miles from my house that offers decent brown trout action. I'd been wanting to catch a respectable brown for a number of years, so I decided to give speed trolling a thorough try during Christmas break.

On the morning of the first day that I'd planned to fish, I almost stayed at home. It had been raining pretty hard for most of the night and according to the morning news the rain wasn't likely to let up. While I didn't relish the idea of setting in the rain all day while trolling from my 12 foot Gregor I knew my chances of hooking a brown trout were really slim if I stayed home and watched television.

After filling my Thermos with coffee, I donned my rain gear and took off for the lake. By the time I arrived at Rollins the precipitation had changed from rain to a dense sloppy slush. The only thing positive about the weather was the fact that the wind wasn't blowing.

Working quickly I stowed my gear and slid the Gregor into the water. Minutes later I zipped away from the launch ramp, cut across the lake's main body and pulled into the Bear River Arm, where most of the lake's browns were rumored to hang out. One of my rods was rigged with a No. 11 floating Rapala in the rainbow trout pattern. A No. 10 silver and black Rapala Husky Jerk was attached to the other rod.

After slowing the boat to 3 miles per hour I free spooled the lures out until they were about 225 feet behind the boat. Putting the rods in their holders I cut the boat in tight to the bank. The shoreline featured a lot of rocky structure, deep drops and fallen trees. It seemed like the type of area where a big brown might be cruising in hopes of ambushing a hapless planter rainbow.

I hadn't gone far, perhaps a quarter mile, when the rod sporting the floating Rapala jerked down into a deep arch and line started shooting off the reel. I figured that I'd snagged some wood, but when I pulled the rod out of the holder and saw the line moving out toward deep water I knew I was into a good fish. Instinctively I hit the tiller and started circling back toward the fish picking up about a hundred feet of line in the process.

With things going my way, I dropped the motor into neutral and settled in for a fight. At first the fish stayed deep, but then without warning it bolted toward bank. Stopping short, it boiled to the surface and I got a brief glimpse of the heavy brown's golden flank before it dove and started shaking its head violently. That's when it happened. I don't know if the trout wasn't hooked well or if it was just plain old bad luck. In any event the line suddenly went slack and I felt as if I'd been kicked in the stomach. In the span of seconds, I'd gone from the highest of highs to the lowest of lows...

I didn't know much about hunting big browns at that point, but I did know that strikes could be far and few between, so I wasn't optimistic about my chances for the rest of the day, but it was way too early to head in. While bass fishing at the lake during the summer, I'd located a long 15 foot deep flat that abruptly dropped into 45 feet of water. The flat was about a half mile away, so I straightened out the boat, got both lines back in the water and started trolling toward the flat with designs on working the transition zone where the flat fell away into deep water.

I'd trolled almost the entire length of the flat before the second brown of the day hit. Instead of going deep the trout ran up onto the flat and tried slugging it out on the surface. Once again I circled back and closed the distance between me and the fish. The trout made two more strong runs, but before long it was swimming right below the boat. In the end, the spring of the rod overcame the strength of the trout and I was finally able to glide the beautiful hook jawed 27 incher into the net. I was elated!

Trophy class brown trout are often heralded as the Holy Grail of trout fishing. Why do big browns hold such an esteemed place in the hearts of trout anglers? I think the answer is twofold. First, brown trout are apex predators that have impressive growth potential. Browns of 10 pounds are common at lakes throughout the west and lunkers in the 20 pound range fall to anglers every year. The all tackle world record, according to the 2012 International Game Fish Association Record Book, weighed 41 pounds 5 ounces. The monster was landed by Roger Hellen of Wisconsin in July 2010. The fish was caught in the Great Lakes system.

Secondly, while big browns may be fairly numerous they are extremely challenging to catch and this undoubtedly accounts for a large measure of their allure. Lake Tahoe provides a good example of just how elusive browns can be. In research done at the lake over the decades it has been determined that brown trout out number rainbows by an approximate ratio of 15 to 1. However, when we look at creel census data the number of rainbows harvested by anglers outdistances the number of browns by approximately 20 to 1. As these numbers illustrate, hooking rainbows is mere child's play compared to hooking browns.

So how does an angler go about hooking browns and more specifically big mature browns? The first requirement is patience, patience and more patience. I hooked two hefty browns on my first attempt, but I assure you that this is the exception rather than the rule. Of course there are periods when all the big browns in a given lake decide to go on the feed and you might get multiple hookups in the span of a few hours. These are the red letter days of brown trout fishing that you never forget. The rest of the time, you'll have to earn your strikes. When I go after rainbows, brookies and mackinaw I seldom get blanked. With browns it's a different story, for every quality brown I hook I'm conscious of the fact that there will be days or even weeks of monotonous trolling, without so much as a tap even though I'm doing everything right.

Trolling for big browns is a game of basics that is more akin to hunting than fishing. To hook a quality brown as with bagging a quality buck, you've got to be in the right place at the right time using the right tactics and when the moment of truth comes you've got to stay cool and execute. To pull this off it is important to have a knowledge of the habits and behaviors of mature brown trout.

Small browns of a pound or less feed primarily on small baitfish, insects and other invertebrates just like rainbows do. As browns increase in size they consistently seek out larger forage items. This is one factor that distinguishes them from other species of trout and accounts for the large sizes they attain. Most of the mature browns that I've cleaned that had forage in their stomachs have either had large baitfish or crawfish inside of them.

While feeding on large prey gives browns a growth advantage, it also makes them all the more difficult to catch. If a fish subsists on a diet of small items it has to spend a good deal of time feeding to stay nourished. Fish such as brown trout that prefer to gulp down large meals only give anglers a narrow window of opportunity, since they are not in a feeding mode the vast majority of the time. Rainbows that earn their living feeding on nymphs or small baitfish can be counted on to feed nearly every day. A big brown, on the other hand, will sweep onto a flat, gobble up a couple planter rainbows and then not feed again for a day or two or three depending on the water temperature. Put a rainbow pattern plug in front of that brown at feeding time and it's hammer time. If the brown has a full belly your chances are greatly diminished.

Since the goal of the brown trout enthusiast is to show them an offering when they are actively hunting for prey it is critical to understand when and where they feed so you can position yourself in the dining room at mealtime. Browns have the reputation for biting best during the late fall, winter and early spring months. Obviously, browns feed just as much in the summer as they do the rest of the year, yet it is during the cool months that they are most accessible to anglers.

Browns are comfortable in water that is 60 degrees or less. In the cool months when surface temperatures are in the 40's and 50's browns will generally be found residing in the top 20 feet of the water column. At such times they show a strong tendency to feed in close proximity to the shoreline. All this translates to the fact that when the surface temperature is cool, anglers can beat the shoreline with top lined offerings, confident in the knowledge that browns will almost certainly see their lures and baits.

Large predatory fish such as brown trout, striped bass and trophy caliber black bass gravitate to shoreline structure during feeding time when the water temperature allows, because operating in relatively shallow water tips the odds of success in their favor. The forage fish these predators target are faster and more maneuverable than they are. If they make their attack in open water the chance of the prey escaping is great. On the other hand if they can box a forage fish in up against shallow shoreline structure such as rip rap, points, fallen trees and boulders their victim can't escape by running toward the structure or by going up or down. To get away they've got to get past the fish that wants to eat them and that greatly increases a small fish's chance of ending up as breakfast, dinner or possibly a light snack!

So far we've established that browns are most vulnerable to anglers during the cool water months when the surface temperature is below 60 degrees. We've also pinned down the fact that when possible, the hook jawed beauties we dream about prefer to feed in shoreline areas that feature ample structure. Our next task is to determine the best time of the day for stalking browns.

Consider if you will, an alley located in a rough neighborhood that is dotted with dumpsters, piles of boxes and recessed doorways. Would you rather walk down that alley in the middle of the day or in the dark? I'm betting that most folks would prefer to make that trip in the middle of the day, so they could see the muggers lurking in the shadows. Well, in a trout lake the browns are the muggers and they are going to be in that alley when the light level is low so they can jump their victims with complete surprise.

The best time to have a close encounter with Mr. Brown is during the first and last hour of daylight and on overcast stormy days when shallow areas are locked in a prolonged period of twilight. Mature browns tend to be very boat shy. Surface chop is often an added advantage that helps minimize the impact of your boat during stormy weather.

Now some anglers may be wondering if fishing at night would give them an advantage. It absolutely would, but the problem is that some lakes don't allow night fishing and even on those that do, the near bank trolling tactics that are used to target browns would likely put both you and your boat in jeopardy.

With a grasp on the when and where, the next question to answer is how, as in how do I get one of those big babies to hit? From what I've read, John Wayne liked to eat steak and drink tequila. If I meet Duke in the Happy Hunting Grounds and invite him over to my place for dinner the menu is going to consist of T-bones and Mescal. The logic is the same when it comes to extending a dinner invitation to a husky brown. Big browns earn their living eating other fish, so trolling with large minnow plugs and rigged dead baitfish is the key to drawing consistent strikes.

To be a successful brown trout troller you don't need to have a huge selection of minnow plugs, but those that you choose have to be high quality baits that run true at both high and low speeds. For decades Rapala minnow plugs were the one and only choice available to trout anglers. These days Rapala floaters and Rapala Husky Jerks continue to be highly effective baits, yet lures from other manufactures have recently joined them in the limelight.

Rapala floaters are constructed of balsa wood. They float on the surface when at rest and dive 4 to 6 feet when trolled. Husky Jerks are made of plastic and boast internal rattles. Jerks dive from 12 to 15 feet when trolled and feature neutral buoyancy. That means that the baits neither float nor sink. If you stop them, as they are being retrieved or trolled they will suspend in the water column.

When I'm after the big boys I don't fool around with small plugs. A peek at my brown trout plug assortment reveals Rapala floaters in both the No. 13 and No. 18 sizes. The No. 13 is 5. 25 inches long while the No. 18 is 7 inches in length.

In terms of colors I try to match what big browns feed on most of the time. Big browns eat a lot of small rainbow trout and they also have a sweet tooth for kokanee salmon wherever the two species coexist. This being the case I carry floaters in the rainbow finish and black over silver. For times when natural finishes aren't working or when the water is stained I like to carry a few bright colored plugs with firetiger being my favorite. Since Husky Jerks don't come in rainbow patterns I carry them in silver over black, glass minnow and fire tiger.

In addition to Rapalas, I employ both Yo-Zuri and River2Sea plugs. My favorite Yo-Zuris are the floating shallow diving F8 Crystal Minnow. This plug is 5. 25 inches long. I also like the floating deep diver R540 Crystal Minnow, which is also 5. 25 inches long. The shallow diver stays in the top 6 feet of water while the deep diver will reach depths in the 20 foot range. As with the Rapalas, I prefer these plugs in the rainbow trout and silver over black finishes.

River2Sea is a well-known lure manufacturer in bass fishing circles, but trout anglers seldom employ their products. This is unfortunate, since their baits exhibit great workmanship and the highest quality components such as needle sharp Daiichi treble hooks. When I'm looking for a certified monster brown I reach for my collection of River2Sea V-Joint Minnows. These suspending plugs come in 3 sizes and feature a unique three section body that gives them a very seductive swimming action. I use the 6. 5 inch 160SU model, which is the largest plug in the V-Joint series. It dives to 8 feet. The V-Joint Minnow boasts a broader body than most other minnow baits and really looks like a substantial meal. Once again my favorite finish is rainbow trout, but I've had success with other finishes too.

The plugs I've discussed are my favorites and I have confidence in them. Having confidence in your baits is critical when targeting big browns, since patience is such an important component to success. It is hard to troll hour after hour while waiting for a strike if you don't have confidence that your lure will draw a hit when you cross paths with a hot fish. Having said that there are number of other fine plugs on the market that anglers swear by. Among the best are AC Plugs, Trophy Sticks and Lucky Crafts. AC's have been taking massive browns for years and I find the Live Pointer series of Lucky Craft baits to be intriguing despite the fact that they are a little small at 4. 5 inches.

I advise new brown trout trollers to start out small in terms of the number of plugs they carry and then gradually build a set of baits that they have supreme confidence in. Knowing what I know now I would start out with a basic selection of Rapalas and learn the ropes of brown trout hunting before adding plugs from other manufacturers to my arsenal to meet specific challenges, which can only be discovered by on the water experimentation.

While Rapalas and other baits are reliable fish producers right out of the package there are a few things an angler can do to enhance their effectiveness. Big browns are almost always old fish and as a result they have experience with a variety of different lures. This is especially true at lakes that have earned the reputation of being top brown trout fisheries, since they attract a lot of hardcore brown trout enthusiasts. In waters that receive a good amount of fishing pressure you are safe in assuming that most of the browns have encountered standard baits such as Rapalas many times. You can overcome their familiarity with these baits through a process I like to call "plug doctoring".

Legendary Lake Tahoe guide Gene St. Denis is a hardcore troller that earns his living by targeting big browns and mackinaws. One of his favorite tactics for enticing big strikes is pulling large minnow plugs, yet you'll never catch Gene using a minnow bait right out of the package. The first thing he does is to scar the bait's finish in various places with a flat file. Next he uses a set of permanent markers to enhance the spots on his baits. He puts black rings around the plugs eyes to make the eyes stand out. A red marker is used to put wide bands of color where the fish's gills would be and he might even put a few red slashes near the bait's tail.

"What I try to do by adding spots to my baits is make them look different from commercially available finishes. The red around the gills makes them look like a panicked fish that is having trouble breathing. When I rough up a bait with my file it makes it look as if it is injured and missing skin. All these changes make the plug look different from anything the trout have seen before and it makes the bait look injured and vulnerable to attack. That's the message you want to convey to a big predator," asserts St. Denis.

I always use Pro-Cure Super Gels in either rainbow trout, herring or sardine scent on minnow plugs to block the scent of my hands and make the baits smell real. You can make your baits taste real by adding a thin herring, shad or sardine fillet to the plug's belly. To accomplish this, fillet a baitfish and then slice the fillet into quarter inch strips. Attach one of these strips along the underside of the minnow plug with the flesh side facing out using fine elastic thread. This is a little known trick that can really pay dividends when dealing with pressured fish. I don't think it makes much difference whether you use shad, sardines or herring. The presence of real meat seems to trigger harder strikes, better hookups and fewer lost trout.

The process for using rigged baitfish for tempting browns is identical to rolling shad, in fact in lakes that feature strong shad populations, rolling large shad is a great way to hook a trophy. In my opinion, an even better option is rolling whole herring. These baits are substantially larger than shad and I'm a strong believer in the "bigger bait equals bigger fish" equation when it comes to bagging a trophy caliber browns. Big browns love to gobble small kokanee in lakes where browns and 'kokes exist together. In waters where it's legal to use them I defy anyone to find a better wounded kokanee imitation than a whole 5 to 6 inch herring rolling through the water.

Before we take a look at the strategies for using plugs and rigged baitfish, let's take a moment to consider the rod and reel necessary for this type of work. Graphite rods have been in vogue among freshwater anglers for a couple decades, yet this is the worst type of rod for brown trout trolling. Instead you want a fiberglass rod. Graphite is super sensitive and resilient when a fish strikes. This is why graphite rods are the best choice for most applications.

Fiberglass rods have a softer action that doesn't react as quickly when subjected to the sudden shock of a striking fish. When trolling plugs with a graphite rod, the plug is often pulled away from the trout at the strike and a missed hookup or a lightly hooked fish is the result. A fiberglass rod is spongier for lack of a better description and this allows the trout to get the plug deeper into its mouth before it feels resistance. Once a trout is hooked, a fiberglass rod does a better job of cushioning a big trout's headshaking fight and this means you'll land more of the fish you hook. My all-time favorite trolling rod for browns is a 7 foot Lamiglas XCF 705. This rod is rated for 10 to 20 pound line and lures up to 1 ounce in weight.

Your rod needs to be teamed with a level wind reel featuring a smooth drag that can handle around 400 yards of 8 pound test line. 8 pound test line has long been the standard line of serious brown trout trollers.

While targeting big browns I adhere to the Gary Miralles formula of starting with a fast presentation and only slowing down when I have to. For many if not all anglers the most consistent approach to hooking large browns is trolling shoreline structure during the cold water months with minnow plugs. The majority of anglers like to troll quickly, but there are some successful anglers out there that experience good results while trolling slowly.

When we talk of trolling quickly for average size rainbow we are talking about speed of 2 to 3 miles per hour. Fast trolling for browns refers to pulling lures at 3 to 5 miles per hour. The first time you drop a plug in the water at these speeds and see how frantically it swims, you'll think there is no way a trout will hit it, but file that thought away. A trout is capable of zipping along at more than 12 miles an hour, so they'll have no problem grabbing a fast moving plug if they want it.

I'm convinced that a speedy presentation results in more strikes because it forces the trout to react quickly. I don't want a big brown following my plug and analyzing its movements. I want the plug to burst on the scene, giving the impression that it is panicked and on the run. A brown trout confronted with such an opportunity has to either react and capitalize on it instantly or let an easy meal escape. Most of the time I troll with my rod in a holder, but at times when my plug is passing near a prime piece of real estate, I'll pick the rod up and work it with staccato pumps. This causes the plug to hesitate and surge, making it even more attractive to any lurking browns.

For me fast trolling is only one piece of the puzzle. Since browns are boat sensitive, the distance the plugs are trolled behind the boat and the way the boat is maneuvered are both highly important. Your plugs should be an absolute minimum of 200 feet behind the boat and on big lakes where conditions allow 400 to 500 feet is even better. I've been out on Lake Tahoe with Gene St. Denis chasing browns and macks when our plugs were a full 400 yards behind the boat due to the water clarity and spookiness of the fish. That's 1,200 feet of line!

Even when the lures are far behind the boat it is still advisable not to drive the boat over prime holding structure whenever possible. Instead of crossing holding areas, swing the boat out around them and then cut the boat back toward the shoreline. This way you can steer the plugs through the honey hole without disturbing it with the boat. One of my favorite structural features to troll is a submerged shelf adjacent to a flat simply because I can troll such locations with very little chance of spooking fish with the boat.

At first I drive the boat offshore of the shelf. When my plugs reach the beginning of the shelf I swing the boat up onto the flat and the plugs swim right over the transition zone. Once I think the plugs are up over the flat I quickly swing back out over deep water, once again putting the plugs on top of the transition zone. With experience, you'll get very adept at using long lines, combined with aggressive boat maneuvering to keep your plugs in virgin water that has not been exposed directly to the boat.

It is important to note that the more familiar you become with any given lake the more effective you'll get at targeting it's browns. Big browns are not spread evenly throughout a lake. Instead they tend to gravitate to specific areas that offer them both shelter and the ability to feed effectively. With time on the water, you'll discover these locations and learn the best ways to cover them without scaring the trout.

Anglers that troll plugs slowly use the same basic approach I've out lined for fast trolling, while traveling between 1. 5 and 3 miles per hour. Yet there is one important exception. The secret weapon of many slow trollers is the use of electric trolling motors and planer boards. The high speed troller can only utilize electric motors for a short period of time before the batteries run low, forcing them to use gas motors most of the time. For the slow troller, electric motors give them the advantage of stealth. This stealth advantage is greatly enhanced by the use of planers since a planer allows them to stay a good distance off shore while trolling the undisturbed water right beside the bank with their lures and baits. This approach is particularly deadly when teamed with a rigged baitfish instead of a plug.

There was a time when I didn't use rigged bait enough when targeting browns. It probably offers an angler the best chance of catching a true heavy weight, but I enjoyed speed trolling so much that it was tough to make the transition.

For anglers that prefer to troll slowly or during the warm water months when the browns go deep and you've got to use downriggers to reach them, rolling shad or herring should be the method of choice. I think the annual spring Kokanee Power team trout and salmon tournament at California's Lake Shasta provides a good example of just how effective rolling baitfish can be when it comes to boating big browns.

The two day tournament attracts some of the most talented guides, anglers and lure manufactures in the west. However, the tournament is seldom won by an angler using lures. You can place in the top 20 and win a prize by catching rainbows and kings, but if you want to win you've got to boat browns and almost every year shad rollers bag those winning browns. I've fished the tournament a number of times. At first I spent a good deal of time pulling plugs amidst the shad rollers, but I've got to confess that I could never come close to matching the effectiveness that they enjoy so now I've joined them!

As a final note on targeting browns, you'll probably keep your first two or three hard won trophies. As you get more effective and refine your approach, consider taking a picture of the big boys you catch and releasing them to fight and spawn again. A big brown has already beaten the odds by reaching a large size and relatively old age. Such a trout deserves our respect and that means releasing them after the battle. Believe me there is something special about looking out across your home lake and knowing there is a big brown swimming around that has your name on it!

Chapter Twenty One: Mackinaw: Underworld Heavyweights

Mackinaw fishing is a lot like sushi. There are those that love it, those that hate it and those that have never tried it. The folks that hate mackinaw contend that while mackinaw can attain great size, they are a boring and tedious fish to pursue due in large measure to the great depths they frequent. These anglers make the case that macks put up a fight that ranges from lethargic at worst to less than spirited at best.

I happen to reside in the camp that loves mackinaw. We love them in part for their unique beauty, the picturesque high mountain lakes they inhabit and the delectable fare they provide when fried, baked or barbequed. But, most of all we love mackinaw for the trophy potential they offer and the challenge involved in first hooking and then landing a true monster.

So just how big do mackinaw get? Well, no one is sure. The current all tackle world record according to the International Game Fish Association as of 2007 stands at 72 pounds. That leviathan was caught by Lloyd Bull while fishing in Canada's Great Bear Lake in August of 1995. Many knowledgeable anglers believe that there are lakers much larger than Bull's lurking in lakes throughout Canada and the western United States. There is a small fraternity of trophy hunters that solemnly hold to the belief that a hundred pound mack cruises the dark recesses of Flaming Gorge Reservoir, Flat Head Lake, Lake Tahoe or in any one of a dozen other trophy mack lakes.

I venture to say that most of us would like to take a run at that record 72 pounder, yet that isn't a goal it's a fantasy. For the average angler fishing in good mackinaw water, a challenging yet attainable goal is a 20 pounder. Lakers weighing over 30 pounds exist at a number of lakes and while one is occasionally hooked it is a rare day when a 30 is landed. These magnificent apex predators are simply too big, too strong and too smart to fall prey to anglers on a regular basis.

I know guides that specialize in targeting big macks that have spent decades fishing some of the west's most productive mackinaw waters without ever landing one beyond the hallowed 30 pound mark. Gene St. Denis is a good example. He earns his dough guiding anglers to trophy macks at Lake Tahoe. Over the past twenty plus years Gene and his clients have bagged more than 40 lakers over 20 pounds, but a 30 pounder has never come into his boat. Yet he and his clients have hooked some monsters that must have been well over 30. On four separate occasions Gene has had big fish sound into deep water spooling him despite the fact that his reels hold more than 200 yards of 20 pound test line!

Deepwater trolling, shallow water trolling and jigging are the three most popular approaches used for subduing macks throughout the year at most western mackinaw lakes, yet before you can fish for them you've got to find them and this can be one of the biggest challenges. Even in lakes that boast a substantial population of macks they can be quite elusive. When it comes to mackinaw the old saying that 90 percent of the fish only occupy 10 percent of the water is scripture. As a result a quality sonar unit is among the most important tools the angler can possess.

As a general guideline, a laker's preferred habitat is craggy boulder strewn ledges that fall into deepwater. If such an area shows signs of forage such as clouds of shrimp, kokanee salmon or chubs the chances of it holding macks increases significantly. During the cold water months from fall through early spring, macks can often be found hunting in shallow bays and on shallow flats. The common denominator that separates productive flats from nonproductive ones is the immediate proximity of deepwater. When the water temperature is cool, mackinaw won't hesitate foraging in shallow areas, so long as the security of deepwater is nearby.

Throughout the year trolling, more specifically deepwater trolling accounts for more mackinaw than shallow water trolling and jigging combined. If your goal is to consistently land limits of average size macks along with the occasional big boy, deepwater trolling in depths ranging from 100 to 350 feet is the way to go. For a generation the only way to get a trolled bait or lure down to these extreme depths was to team steel line with hefty lead weights. While some deepwater specialists still employ steel line, the vast majority of today's anglers employ downriggers.

Uninitiated anglers often assume that since they successfully pull rainbows out of deepwater using their downriggers the same approach will earn them a quick limit of macks, but this is seldom the case. While the basics of downrigger trolling are the same no matter what species is being targeted there are a number of variations in both tactics and tackle that differentiate the successful rainbow troller from the troller that consistently boats macks.

When targeting rainbows it is often to the angler's benefit to cover ground, while the exact opposite is often true when it comes to hooking lakers residing in deepwater.

A successful mackinaw troll begins with pinpointing a group of fish using sonar and marking their position using a GPS unit. Generally speaking, mackinaw holding just off the bottom are the easiest to catch because they tend to stay put, allowing the angler to work on them. Deep water macks may or may not be actively feeding, but provided the fish stay in one position they can often be caught even if they aren't in a feeding mode initially. You see, inactive fish can often be prodded into feeding, by presenting your baits to them multiple times. I'll talk more about this a little later, but first let's consider the tackle needed for deepwater mackinaw hunting.

While most of the macks caught in deepwater will range from 3 to 6 pounds, it is important to employ a rod and reel that will handle lakers in the 10 to 20 pound range when one of these trophies decides to strike. A 7 foot medium action casting rod rated for 10 to 20 pound line is ideal for mackinaw trolling. Macks have soft mouths and tend to nip at baits and lures rather than engulfing them. This means that most of the time the fish will be lightly hooked. If a fast action rod is employed you'll lose a lot of fish due to hooks being pulled out. A medium action rod, owing to the softness of its tip is more forgiving and will enable you to bring more fish to the boat.

The rod should be teamed with a high speed level wind casting reel with a 4. 5 to 1 or better retrieve ratio. The reel needs to be capable of holding 200 to 250 yards of 15 or 17 pound monofilament. A smooth reliable drag is a critical component for landing big macks, so it is important to purchase the best quality reel your budget will allow.

Some anglers might be tempted to load their reel with braided line, but this is a mistake. Braid stretches very little and as a result it is not very forgiving. Much like using a fast action rod, braided line will result in more fish pulling loose. Monofilament features a good deal of stretch and this tends to cushion the surges and headshakes of a feisty laker.

With a rod and reel in hand, it's time to talk about the baits, lures and blades used for tempting deepwater lakers. The first thing the aspiring mack hunter needs to pick up is a small assortment of large dodgers and a set of big flashers for each downrigger. The color of the dodgers isn't a huge factor, but I favor dodgers that are adorned with glow in the dark paint or tape. There are a number of effective dodgers on the market from manufactures such as Sep's Pro Fishing, Lure Jensen and the Shasta Tackle Company. I prefer Shasta Tackle's Magnum Sling Blade because it works well at both high and low speeds with a little bending.

Mackinaw, particularly those residing in deepwater will hit a variety of different offerings. Rigged baitfish are a top choice wherever it's legal to use them. A lot of dedicated mackinaw specialists go through the trouble of catching chubs and other minnows that are native to the lakes they fish. I've always done well using the 2 to 3 inch shiners that are found in bait shops as well as frozen herring that are most commonly used by ocean salmon trollers.

Some anglers insist that it is crucial to have live minnows, but I have never found this to be the case. Since the common method for rigging minnows for trolling is to thread a treble hook tipped leader through the body of the baitfish, I doubt if it makes much difference whether the minnow is alive or fresh frozen.

For small minnows I typically use a No. 6 treble attached to a 16 inch piece of 15 pound monofilament leader. I thread the leader through the minnow from the vent to the mouth such that the treble rides along the bottom of the bait just in front of the tail. When using herring or other large baitfish I go with the same leader length, but I upsize the treble to a No. 2 or 4. When using baitfish I always pull them behind a dodger or set of flashers.

At times when I don't have or can't use baitfish, I've found Shasta Tackle's large double hook Kok-A-Nuts, Matrix Minnows and plastic Matrix Paddle Tails to be effective substitutes. The Matrix Paddle Tail is basically a small minnow imitating soft plastic bait. I rig them just like I rig a real baitfish, using one of my treble hook tipped leaders. Kok-A-Nuts and Matrix Minnows are flies that provide a lot of flash and movement. I also like to rig them behind a dodger.

Other effective baitfish substitutes include grubs from Berkley and Sep's as well as Hoochies from P-Line, Gold Star and others.

Most of the time rigged baitfish, soft plastics and flies are all I need to hook up, but once in a while deepwater macks show a strong preference for plugs. For these situations I always have a few Yo-Zuri Crystal Minnows, floating Rapala Minnows, broken back Bomber Long A's and EChip equipped Pro Troll Sting Kings on hand. I don't think the color makes a big difference when it comes to selecting plugs for use in deepwater, but since macks like to feed on small rainbow trout and kokanee salmon I almost always go with rainbow trout and silver over black pattern plugs. When using plugs I run them alone without dodgers.

Once you get on the water for a deepwater trolling session the first task is to locate a group of fish holding near the bottom using the sonar unit. When you get some promising looking returns, mark the location of the fish on your GPS and get ready to drop your rigs down to them. If I have baitfish they are my first choice, followed by my soft plastics, flies and finally plugs.

Since deepwater macks will likely be sluggish when you first show them your lures I heavily scent all my offerings. A number of different scents work well including rainbow trout, sardine, herring, trophy trout, shrimp, krill and garlic. Not only do I apply the scent to the bait, but I also smear it on my dodgers too. Naturally the scent is intended to draw strikes from individual macks, but as you make multiple passes through the fish it also creates a cloud of scent that helps to excite the whole pack.

With your lures doused with scent it's time to drop those offerings down to the fish and go to work. Since you'll be working in deepwater your rigs only need to be between 15 to 25 feet behind the downrigger weight. Staying on the fish and triggering them to strike requires a lot of maneuvering. If you put too much line behind the downriggers, your rigs will have a tendency to tangle. Generally when dealing with bottom hugging fish I'll start off trolling a foot or two above them.

Deep water trolling is not a high speed affair. With baitfish, plastics and flies, speeds between . 8 and 1. 5 miles per hour are perfect. When using plugs you can push the speed up to 2 or at most 2. 5. Trolling for deep dwelling macks is unlike any other trout trolling, since your goal is to troll a very small patch of the bottom while working in conjunction with your sonar and GPS. You want to maneuver in circles and figure eights, keeping the lures in front of the fish as much as possible.

Of course we all want immediate action when we mark fish on our sonar units and drop lures down to them, but this often won't be the case when you first start working a pod of macks. Over the years I've found that macks will often give you the cold shoulder at first. After I work the fish for 10 to 20 minutes I start getting a few tentative strikes and the bite builds from there.

Many times I've struggled to get my first strike and by the time I'm finished working a pod the bite is wide open. Why? Well, first of all I believe that repeatedly showing the macks my lures aggravates them and causes them to become more active. The Pro-Cure scents I use are infused with bite stimulating amino acids that encourage the fish to feed. Finally, when a mack is hooked they almost always regurgitate everything in their stomach. I know it sounds pretty nasty, but the spit up food acts as chum for the rest of the pack.

When the macks are playing particularly hard to get, it often pays to bounce the bottom with your downrigger weights. This creates vibration and raises the silt, which both act as strong stimulants for drowsy deep water lakers. Bottom bouncing is clearly a risky move in that you could easily snag your weights, yet this tactic is one of the closely guarded secrets of both guides and dedicated mackinaw experts. Bottom bouncing is not something you want to try in a rocky craggy area. The key is to become familiar enough with the function of your sonar unit to identify whether the bottom is rough snaggy rock or relatively smooth gravel or sand.

Gary Coe is one of the west coast's most talented kokanee salmon trollers. While he doesn't often fish for macks, he does spend a lot of time bouncing the bottom to draw strikes from the diminutive salmon he loves to catch. Instead of using round or pancake shaped downrigger weights he makes his own out of solid rods of stainless steel. The result is a long skinny weight that won't wedge between rocks the way a round weight will.

Okay so you are trolling, the lures and scent are working and a fish decides to strike. Even smallish macks are big heavy fish compared to the rainbows we often catch, so the mack is going to pull the line right out of the downrigger clip, right? Well, sometimes that is exactly how a strike occurs, but more often than not a bite is much subtler than that. Since your offerings are moving slowly lakers tend to nip at them daintily and get hooked right in the front of the mouth. Many times when they are hooked they will swim along with the boat and the line won't be pulled from the release.

As a result it is imperative to keep watching your rod tips as you troll. A few light taps or pumps are often the only things that register a hooked fish. If you think a fish is on the bait, grab the rod, pop the line out of the clip and reel as quickly as you can to get the slack out of the line. Once the mack feels the resistance and is drawn off the bottom it will wake up, shift gears and begin putting up the dogged head shaking fight that deepwater macks are known for.

Since most deepwater fish are lightly hooked you want to avoid pumping the rod, as this will pull the hooks free. Instead keep he rod tip up and focus on reeling smoothly and steadily. Once you work the fish up out of the depths its swim bladder will expand and it will balloon up to the surface.

If you release a fish with an expanded air bladder it will float on the surface and die. For a successful release the air in the bladder needs to be drained off using the tip of a hypodermic needle. If the bladder can be seen protruding from the mouth of the mack you can puncture it there and use your fingers to gently squeeze out the air. If the bladder is not protruding you'll need to carefully insert the needle into the bulged abdomen and use finger pressure to coax out the gas. Once such a fish is deflated, revive it and then shove it head first into the water.

While these procedures sound pretty brutal, long term mackinaw tagging performed by Mickey Daniels of Mickey's Big Mack Charters at Lake Tahoe indicates that a large percentage of fish released in this manner survive.

"I've tagged and released a number of fish that looked to be in pretty bad shape, yet I've caught several of them years later that looked as healthy as any other fish," discloses Daniels.

Another popular and productive method for targeting deep water lakers is jigging. Jigging is an effective method for catching most types of gamefish when they are tightly schooled. In the case of mackinaw, jigging works all year long, but is most effective in the late summer and early fall. This is when the fish bunch up, as they get ready to spawn.

Jigging is really pretty simple. It refers to yo-yoing a lure up and down in an area known to hold fish. When it comes to mackinaw jigging you want to cruise around, locate and record the location of a school or pod on your GPS. The next step is to drop a Cripple Herring Spoon, Gibbs Minnow Spoon or a bucktail jig down to the level of the fish, generally just above the bottom and begin working it up and down with long smooth strokes of the rod tip. If you want you can mix things up with some shorter pumps, jabs and pauses, but a steady smooth jigging motion will almost always draw strikes.

The weight of the lure you employ is dependent on the depth of the water and the speed you are drifting. If conditions are dead calm and the fish are holding in 100 feet of water you might get by with a 2 ounce lure. If the water is deeper or if a breeze is pushing the boat you might have to increase the weight of the lure to 3, 4 or 5 ounces.

For added enticement the jigs should be slathered with Pro-Cure Super Gel in the same scents used for trolling. Many anglers tip their jigs with pork rind or plastic trailers. For the ultimate attraction I like to tip my jigs with a minnow or a herring fillet. If you have trouble keeping a herring fillet attached to your jig and you are using metal spoon type jigs you should consider attaching a fillet on the side of the jig using elastic thread with the flesh side out. This will put off scent as well as small bits of meat. When a mack grabs it, will taste like a genuine baitfish.

Jigging rods and lines differ significantly from those used for trolling. The rod should be constructed out of sensitive graphite and should feature a fast action. Meaning it should possess a sensitive pliable tip followed up by solid backbone. As we discussed, monofilament is great for the troller because it features stretch. Stretch is just what you don't want while jigging and that is why most avid jiggers now employ braided super lines.

Braided lines feature virtually no stretch and as a result they are super sensitive enabling you to easily feel the bottom and the strikes of cooperative fish. Braids also have a much better strength to diameter ratio as compared to monofilament. For example 30 pound braid has a diameter smaller than 10 pound monofilament. This means that braid offers less water resistance than monofilament and as a result you'll be able to get down with less weight. This will result in more hookups over the course of the season.

There are a number of superb braids on the market. My personal favorites include Berkley Fireline and Spiderwire Ultracast as well as braids from P-Line and McCoy. Generally I use 30 pound braid, but a lot of anglers prefer to use 20 or even 15 pound test. Regardless of the breaking strength of the braid you use, you'll want to tip it with a high quality swivel. Attach a 30 inch 15 to 20 pound test monofilament or fluorocarbon leader to the swivel and then tie on your jig using a loop knot to give it maximum action.

Most anglers unfamiliar with jigging assume that strikes will occur on the upstroke, but that is seldom the case. Jigs are most often hit as they sink, so you want to try to stay in touch with the bait as it drops. This way if you feel a tap or if it hesitates you'll be ready to hammer the hook home.

When you feel or sense something and set the hook, fight the temptation to stand there like a statue with the rod tip held high to see if you've hooked up. If there is a mack on the line, particularly a big one this hesitation on your part is all the advantage they need to shake the hook. When you set the hook immediately start cranking reel. If there is a fish down there the rod will load up and pull the hook into the macks mouth beyond the barb.

Okay, we've pulled plenty of keeper size macks out of deepwater and they sure did provide some great eating, but now it is time to go hunting for trophies and that means top lining with magnum minnow plugs and swimbaits. My passion is big fish and this is the type of mackinaw fishing that really gets my heart pumping.

Just the mention of big mackinaw dredges up memories of a trip I took with Gene St. Denis and my father in law Gene Rush during the spring. St. Denis told me that he'd located a group of big macks patrolling a flat on Tahoe's western shoreline and he'd been hooking fish in the 10 to 20 pound class while long lining No. 18 rainbow pattern Rapalas. Naturally I wasted no time accepting his invitation to fish. A day later Gene and I found ourselves waiting for St. Denis to arrive at the Cave Rock launch ramp in the predawn darkness. I'd brought along a few big Rapalas for St. Denis and I also packed a massive River2Sea V-Joint minnow plug that I'd been field testing for stripers and black bass.

After St. Denis arrived we shot across the lake in his Alumaweld and lined up for our first troll across the flat. Two rods sported rainbow Rapalas and one was armed with the rainbow pattern River2Sea bait. It didn't take us long to start hooking "small" fish in the 8 to 10 pound class. We were top lining our baits a full 400 yards behind the boat on 8 pound test line to overcome Tahoe's gin clear water and the spooky nature of big macks holding in shallow water.

We'd made about a half dozen passes across the long flat when the rod armed with the V-Joint pulled down into a deep arch and Gene pulled it out of the rod holder. "That's a big fish. We'll be lucky if we ever lay our eyes on it," commented St. Denis as line ripped off the reel. Finally a few minutes later the big mack slowed down and St. Denis started maneuvering the boat, so Gene could gain back some line. About 15 or 20 minutes into the fight Gene had all the line save for about 150 feet back on the reel. The big fish had dropped down into about 100 feet of water and was content swimming along lazily to the side of the boat. Gene tried to bring the big fish up, but it refused to budge.

From time to time it would rocket forward, pulling several yards of line off the reel, which Gene would slowly regain. At other times the laker would stop dead in the water and shake its head violently. Gene had been fighting the fish for well over a half hour when it shook its head and tossed the hook. St. Denis's prediction turned out to be correct, we never caught a glimpse of the mack.

Gene was momentarily crushed. It was by far the largest trout he'd ever hooked and it was gone after a tantalizing long fight. "That fish would have gone over 20," St. Denis told us as we put the lines back out. On the day our top fish weighed in at 12 pounds, which is nothing to sneeze at, but we lost three after prolonged fights that St. Denis felt confident were in the high teens or low 20's. At the end of a day like that if you're not hooked on top lining for trophy macks you should give up fishing and take up golf!

The basic techniques used when top lining for macks are simple and straight forward, but the most important ingredient for success can't be found in a tackle store. It is something that resides inside the angler. I'm talking about patience. In the big picture it takes a good deal of patience and a stick to it attitude to locate, hook and land trophy caliber macks residing in the shallows.

Of course the first challenge for the top liner is locating a productive fishing area. Spring and fall are the prime times for top lining because this is the time of the year when the surface temperature on most mackinaw lakes is in the middle to upper 40's at these times big macks that spend most of the year holding in isolated deepwater areas, move onto shallow water structure and hunt for prey in the form of chubs, small rainbows, small mackinaw, wayward kokanee and crawfish.

Classic areas for locating macks at such times include, long boulder dotted flats that abruptly drop into deepwater, long points that gradually fall into deepwater and large expanses of shallow to moderately deep water say from 20 to 50 feet deep, that are punctuated by deep dips and holes where macks can hold and race up to attack smaller fish swimming overhead. In such areas your sonar's primary value comes in reading the contour of the bottom rather than actually spotting fish. If you spot small fish cruising shallow areas or if you mark macks holding on a drop adjacent to a shallow water feeding area there is a good chance that you'll stumble across big macks cruising for a meal.

The best time for plying such areas is during periods of low light such as dawn, dusk and on over cast days, yet it is possible to hook big macks all day long while top lining when the water temperature is right even when the sun is directly overhead. Top lining when the sun is high in the sky is at its slowest when the water is dead calm. It really helps the troller's cause if there is a breeze providing some surface chop to help diffuse the sunlight.

All things considered if I'm really out for a trophy I'd have to say that a stormy overcast day that blankets the lake with chop and small whitecaps is prime time for encountering a true heavy weight, yet we've got to play the cards we are dealt and fish when our schedules allow.

The same types of rods and reels that are used for downrigger fishing can be used for top lining, but the heavy line has to be replaced with 400 to 550 yards of 8 pound test line. Now I know that it seems crazy to go with light line when you are in search of massive 10 to 20 plus pound fish, but you've got to consider the quarry. Mackinaw typically inhabit clean clear lakes and they almost always attack top lined lures from below. If your line is too heavy the fish will see it silhouetted against the light of the sky and that will cost you strikes.

In most lakes mackinaw grow slowly, so big fish are generally pretty old. These old timers have seen it all and have probably been hooked and lost. When such fish see something out of place, such as heavy line coming off a perspective prey item they usually pass it up rather than take a chance.

Another reason for using such small line is line capacity. Mackinaw spend most of their time holding in deepwater where it's quiet. When they are in the shallows they feel vulnerable. As a result they avoid the vibrations and noises put off by boats. This means that in order to get strikes consistently from trophy caliber fish the lure has to be from 200 to 400 yards away from the boat depending on the size and configuration of the lake.

It doesn't take an extensive collection of lures to take macks while top lining. Macks, like the large browns we discussed in Chapter 9, have a weakness for grabbing minnow plugs because they mimic the prey items that lakers are accustomed to eating. The minnow plugs I use for targeting lakers are identical to those I use when prospecting for browns. While fishing lakes that hold both species, it is common to catch browns while targeting macks and equally common to hook macks while chasing browns.

In short my plug selection for mackinaw top lining consists of Rapala floaters in both the No. 13 and No. 18 sizes. I carry these in both rainbow trout finish for imitating small rainbows and black over silver to imitate kokanee. Since the floating Rapalas dive from 4 to 6 feel, I also add a few No. 14 Rapala Husky Jerks in black over silver and glass minnow. Husky Jerks run from 12 to 15 feet deep. Beyond the Rapalas, I carry the same Yo-Zuri Crystal minnows and River2Sea V-Joint minnows in the same sizes and colors that I mentioned using for browns in the previous chapter.

One plug that I don't routinely use for browns, but I do employ for macks is a River2Sea Wood 'N' Slither swimbait in the rainbow trout finish. This is a triple jointed black bass bait with a rubber tail. The bait has a broad profile and a seductive swimming action when pulled slowly through the water. The Wood 'N' Slither runs right under the surface so I only used it in super shallow water or when the light level is low. This swimbait won't draw as many strikes as a Rapala, but if it comes within range of a truly huge mack that is on the prowl for its next meal, it's Fish On Baby!

For me big brown trolling is best done at relatively high speeds, but when looking for big macks I like to back my speed off some and run between 2. 5 and 3. 5 mile per hour. Gene St. Denis believes that macks will follow plugs pulled at a steady rate for great distances without striking. For this reason he constantly speeds up and slows down. One of his favorite tactics it is to drop his reel into free spool every now and then. He feels that when the plug goes dead in the water any following mack will over run it and strike at it. According to St. Denis, it is surprising how many times when you re-engage the reel a few seconds later that there will be a mackinaw at the end of the line.

A lot of anglers believe it is a waste of time to use scents when top lining, but St. Denis disagrees. "When a big mack comes up and follows your lure you want to use everything you can to encourage the fish to strike. I never top line without adding scent to my lures. I firmly believe that when a trout is moving in on my lures that scent can be the difference between closing the deal and having the fish turn away without committing," says St. Denis.

Like St. Denis I am a believer in scents. I know that at worst, using scent isn't going to hurt and it will likely get me more strikes than I would get without it. I like to use the same Pro-Cure Super Gels I use when trolling deep or jigging.

Okay! Picture the scene. You're in your boat working a shallow flat. The sky is overcast and you're towing a big minnow plug 300 yards behind the boat. Suddenly the rod bends violently and line starts pulling off the reel. There is a big fish on the line, what will you do next?

The first thing you want to do is stay calm. Take the rod out of the holder and drop the motor into neutral. Let the fish run with the rod tip held high. When your prize stops running start working the reel to ensure the line stays tight and drop the motor back into gear. As you use the reel to keep the line tight, circle back toward the fish out over deepwater. This will enable you to gain back line and coax the fish out over deepwater where there is less chance of it wrapping the line around a snag. You don't want to crowd the fish, but it is important to use the motor to keep the fish out to the side or behind the boat.

The worst thing you can do is try to rush the fight. Just keep the rod high and work the reel to keep the line tight. Most macks won't engulf the plug and as a result they are generally lightly hooked, but you can land a good percentage of them with calm nerves and a light drag. When you work the big boy to the boat the first time you can almost always count on it taking off on a power dive. This is when novice anglers often loose big macks. If you know it is going to happen, you'll be ready for it. After the initial dive you'll usually be able to work it back up to the boat in a minute or two or three. It may be ready to net or it may dive again. Just stick with it and don't try to net the fish if its head is down. When it comes to the surface with its head up it's time to make your move with the net and bring the monster into the boat.

When you beat the odds and land your first big laker the feeling of exhilaration and accomplishment you feel will be the basis for a lifelong memory and of course you won't be able to get your gear back in the water fast enough so you can do it all over again.

As a final thought most anglers keep the first big mack they land. After that please consider releasing the big 15 plus pounders you catch. Such fish are old and they deserve to live to fight another day, plus smaller fish in the 5 to 10 pound range provide much better table fare.

Chapter Twenty Two: Trout Eat Minnows, But Keep That Under Your Hat...

That's right loose lips sink ships! Big fish eat little fish and trout be they browns, brookies or 'bows living in streams, lakes or reservoirs all gobble minnows with gusto. But let's keep this information between you and I or everyone and their brother will be casting and pulling plugs and scoring big trout. And after all we want those hook jawed, slob gutted minnow munchers for ourselves, right?

At this point you probably think I'm talking about ripping big minnow plugs like size 13 and 18 floating Rapalas. While fast trolling big baits like these is a tried and true approach for hooking trophy size fish, that's not what I'm focusing on. Fishing these magnum size plugs for trout is a bit like sturgeon fishing, the hookup and fights are awesome, but the waiting time between bites can be long and tedious.

What we want to consider are smaller minnow plug and crankbaits that will catch trout of all sizes. Plugs in the one to three inch range are small enough to tempt pan size trout, but when you come across a big girl these plugs are substantial enough that she just won't be able to pass them up.

It wasn't long ago that John Merwin in the pages of Outdoor Life rated minnow plugs third in the list of all-time best trout lures and if Outdoor Life says something it must be true!

In all seriousness, I don't think any trout angler whether they fish streams or lakes from the bank or from a boat should be without a selection of minnow plugs, but they are only part of the story when it comes to trout plugs.

Short thick bodied bass fishing style crankbaits and boomerang shaped plugs like Kwikfish and Flatfish should also be part of the well-heeled trouter's arsenal. I never seem to have enough room in this column, so let's quickly go over lures selection, tackle and fishing tactics relating to the category of lures that I refer to as "trout plugs".

I like to fish my plugs on 8-pound fluorocarbon line. If I'm fishing a stream or casting at a lake I go with spinning gear. If I'm trolling, a conventional rig utilizing a level wind baitcaster gets the nod. Whether I'm using spinning or conventional tackle I like a rod with a soft tip. Trout have soft mouths and the soft tip helps to minimize lost fish.

My plug selection for fishing creeks and rivers is smaller than the selection I carry for lake and reservoir fishing. On the stream I like size 5 and 7 floating Rapalas in rainbow trout, silver/black and firetiger or orange. If the stream I'm fishing is exceptionally deep and swift I'll sometimes add a few count down Rapalas to my selection, but as a general rule I've found that deep holding trout have no problem coming up to smack a Rapala working overhead.

For crankbaits, I rely on Shasta Tackle Flee Bitties, small Hotshots and Brad's Wigglers in rainbow trout and orange over gold. When it comes to Kwikfish or Flatfish I like to have baits in red, frog and chrome/blue.

While all of these bait imitate minnows I fish them all differently. I use my Rapalas to cover water quickly. I cast them across and slightly down stream, allow them to swing across the current on a tight line and then retrieve them slowly. After one or two casts I move downstream a few feet and repeat. This approach works best in streams that are reasonably open that allow me to cover the water thoroughly and quickly.

I still use Rapalas on brushy streams, but in general I use crankbaits and boomerang plugs more. Since heavy brush prevents you from effectively walking and casting you have cover a lot of water from each opening in the brush. To accomplish this I tie on a crankbait and pitch it out a few feet into the middle of the current and close the reel's bail. The plug will immediately swim to the near bank. I allow it to work there for several seconds and then begin feeding it line a foot or two at a time, giving it plenty of pauses to sit and work in the current. It's amazing how many trout will dart out from under the bank and absolutely slam the bait.

If crankbaits don't produce in this situation I tie on a Kwikfish or Flatfish and fish it the same way except I add a 10 inch section of 8 pound fluorocarbon tipped with a No. 10 woolly bugger to the eye where the lure's rear hook attaches. The plug acts as an attractor/diver. About half the fish will be hooked on the fly while the other half will hammer the plug.

When bank fishing lakes or reservoirs my plug selection doesn't change. Key locations to fish are points and anywhere water is flowing into the lake. These areas should be thoroughly worked via fan casting. In lakes where the main forage is shad, I like to employ crankbaits and boomerang plugs most of the time. If pond smelt are on the menu Rapalas tend to work better, but of course this is just a general rule. In reality Rapalas work just about everywhere.

And now we come to trolling. One of the reasons I really like minnow plugs and crankbaits for trolling is that they are baits that I can work quickly. Typically I troll them from 2 to 3 miles per hour. These baits work equally well when top lined or trolled from downriggers. When top lined you'll want the plugs at least 150 feet behind the boat with 200 feet being preferable. When pulling them behind a downrigger you can shorten up significantly, although I still like to keep them at least 50 feet behind the ball.

If fast trolled plugs don't do the trick, breakout a Flatfish or Kwikfish. This style of lure was used extensively by our fathers, but trout in lakes and reservoirs don't see them that much anymore, which is great...Curiosity killed the cat...er rainbow!

Boomerang plugs work best when pulled from 1 to 1. 5 mph. If you want to get tricky don't be afraid to pull the same woolly bugger trick I described for stream fishing. Sometimes it works well especially at locations like Eagle Lake and Lake Davis where the fish eat a lot of bugs.

Let's wrap things up by considering color selection. All things being equal I like to run with natural colored offerings like rainbow trout or black over silver. When the water is murky that's when I break out the firetiger and hot orange colors, yet there are always exceptions. I get a lot of photos working at the Fish Sniffer and a lot of huge trout are landed in crystal clear lakes like Pardee, Almanor and French Meadows on bright orange Rapalas.

A buddy of mine just took a trip to Pardee and asked me what he should troll with. I told him I'd mess around with grubs, Cripplures and Uncle Larry's spinners tipped with worms, but added that I'd have an orange Rapala in the water all the time. I told him he probably wouldn't catch anything on it, but there is always the chance that he'd be the next guy to pull a 10 plus pound brown out of the lake!

Chapter Twenty Three: Slinging Roe For Trout!

Late fall and early winter and synonymous with trout fishing, that's a given. But how do you go about hooking those trophy browns and rainbows?

For a long time I was only aware of a couple of different tried and true methods. If you had access to a boat fast trolling with minnow plugs or slow trolling or "rolling" rigged baitfish are solid approaches.

For bank anglers, plugging with the same minnow plugs that trollers use or soaking inflated crawlers produce results for patient anglers.

A few years ago, while talking with north state trout guru Doug Neal of Almanor Fishing Adventures a new trophy trout method popped onto my radar screen. Neal employs trout roe for tempting both trophy caliber browns and hefty rainbows. Using trout roe makes perfect sense, yet very few anglers have ever heard of the method.

Before I explain how "roeing for trout works" let's explore why it is such an effective approach. Browns residing in lakes and reservoirs gravitate toward tributaries in the fall and early winter. Browns are fall/winter spawners and they will ultimately surge into these tributaries to complete the spawn process.

In the days and weeks before spawning activity actually occurs, the browns stack up around the mouth of the tributaries. Often times large rainbows will be found in the same area, drawn there by the opportunity to gobble up wayward eggs once spawning takes place.

Both before and during the spawn, both browns and rainbows will enthusiastically pounce on a well presented piece of roe. Salmon eggs will work and so will salmon roe, but not nearly as well as the real thing. You need trout roe!

You can't buy trout roe, so you've got to harvest it yourself. Basically you need to find the areas where the browns are stacking up and catch one of them. Short of having trout roe, one of the best offerings you can employ is a natural colored Pautzke salmon egg. It's not trout roe, but with persistence it will work.

We'll talk about how to present roe and salmon eggs at the end of this chapter, but at this point let's pretend that you've caught a female brown. You don't want to keep a really large fish, because it is important that those fish are allowed to spawn. For the sake of this chapter we'll say that you've landed a fat 3 or 4 pounder.

The first thing you want to do is stun the trout and then cut its gills. You want to drain the trout's blood so it can't pool up in the roe. Once the trout has been bled, carefully slice the fish open and extract the roe skeins without damaging them.

There are hundreds of secret cures in use these days and dozens of established commercial cures on the market, yet Fire Cure is one of the most effective and simplest cures you can employ.

The folks at the Pautzke Bait Company teamed up with dry cure specialist Mark Yano to produce Fire Cure.

Yano, originally from Hawaii, spent his youth pursuing saltwater fish but quickly turned into a freshwater fanatic after moving to Oregon in 1980. In 1981, Yano mastered his own egg cure formula, "Yano Cure," which quickly became a Northwest favorite. Now, Yano and Pautzke Bait Co. have teamed up to produce the most effective curing formula available. Combining Pautzke's world-renowned knowledge in egg science and proven secret seasonings with Yano's formula and curing technique makes Fire Cure a necessity for all anglers.

"Fire Cure is special due to the consistency of the cure. You don't get one batch that's too hot and then one batch that's less hot than the other. It's perfect all the time," notes Casey Kelley, President of Pautzke Bait Company, the world leader in salmon eggs. "We've got just the right amount of krill attractant and specific coloring. I can't say why it's the perfect cure because I don't want to get into talking about each specific ingredient that makes it so perfect, but hands down, it's an easy to use cure that helps change the average roe into excellent roe that's a must have for salmon. "

Whether in Alaska, the Pacific Northwest, the California Coast or in the Upper Sacramento Valley, the race to find the hottest and greatest cure is constantly on the mind of salmon, steelhead and trout anglers. Oftentimes, anglers with the best roe out duel their competitors.

"Geez, I used to use Pro Cure and I used to use Atlas, but then we broke an old recipe out of the book and teamed up with Mark Yano, who had a base formula that was unlike any other out there. We added some key Pautzke family ingredients and now we have Fire Cure, the hottest cure on the market," explained Kelley. "Whether it was us or someone else that comes out with a new cure I think people are always looking for the next best cure. Ours is so dang easy to use and so effective that it's become very popular among anglers and guides alike. "

Twenty plus year veteran Northern California salmon and steelhead guide Wally Johnson said Fire Cure is like no cure he's stumbled upon before.

"I like the fact that it has the krill in it already. It puts the eggs at the color I like to have them. The bright eggs are really important and it makes a nice, tight egg cluster that holds together on the hook," says Johnson. "I think the krill in Fire Cure is the ticket. That's my feeling. The krill gives it that extra scent that I think makes a lot of difference in how many fish you catch. I've tested it a lot. I've taken other roe with other cures and put it side by side and the Fire Cure out fishes it. When I fish the Klamath, the Smith, The Chetco and the Sacramento River when I'm salmon fishing I have the Fire Cure eggs. "

Fire Cure is a sulfite cure, rather than a borax cure. Historically, sulfite cures are more effective on salmon and trout, especially in California. Some anglers in the Pacific Northwest use borax cures for salmon eggs as well.

"Fire Cure to me has a really good sulfite and sweet smell to it. I used to mix up a secret cure that I thought worked better than a lot of cures, but once Fire Cure came out it worked as well or better and now that's why I use it," noted longtime Sacramento, Feather and American River guide JD Richey. "It is really easy to use and Wally Johnson is right, the krill in the cure is powerful and Fire Cure is almost fool proof to use. The thing I like about Fire Cure is the fish seem to really like it. That's the big bottom line, fish just love Fire Cure. Generally speaking, the rule to thumb is you use sulfite based cure for salmon and the thought is steelhead don't like sulfite as much, but I've found the steelhead like the Fire Cure too. "

Longtime Red Bluff and Redding area guide Mike Bogue is another that's sold on Fire Cure.

"I think the eggs hold together better than any other cure I've ever used and I love the krill smell on them. It gives those eggs a more potent smell as opposed to any other cure," explains Bogue. "When I use red Fire Cure the eggs they don't spade near as quickly as some of the other cures and it's very easy to use. A guy that's new to curing eggs can definitely find Fire Cure very easy to use. "

Anglers who cure eggs often are aware of the risks. Many cures, if not used carefully can destroy quality eggs. On the other hand, Fire Cure makes the curing process so simple that the absolute beginner can pull it off with professional results! If you can make something as simple as coffee you can get great results using Fire Cure...just follow the directions!

With many sulfite cures the problem you have is you have to baby sit the eggs so much. If you don't watch your eggs carefully, you'll overcook or burn your eggs. Burned eggs are over-dehydrated. The nice thing about the Pautzke's Fire Cure is that the balance of the sulfite in it gives you a bigger window of error, making it much easier to achieve successful results.

Fire Cure is available in four colors: natural, red, pink and orange. Each color has a purpose. Natural is best applied to eggs you want to stay in their natural state. Since no die is added to natural its best used when you are going to fish your egg in low, clear water conditions. Pink and orange are applied to eggs when there's color to the water. Red is the most popular color and tends to be effective under all water conditions.

Another great aspect of Fire Cure is the color is balanced. The color pigments in the die Pautzke uses disperse better and more evenly throughout the skein than with other cures.

To end up with a good egg, you must start with a good egg. Bleed your fish immediately and don't let the eggs touch water. After removing the eggs place them in paper towels, put them in a large plastic bag and put them on ice. You'll need to cure them within 36 hours for the best results.

For best results, cover curing surface with newspaper, then cover with paper towels. Cut skeins in half, then into 1 to 2 inch pieces and lay flat on paper towel. Generously sprinkle Fire Cure on both sides of skein then layer skeins in a wide mouth jar or other sealed container. Secure lid then label with date of cure and type of egg. Store at room temperature for one hour, periodically rolling the jar to ensure the cure completely dissolves in the juice being released from the eggs. Refrigerate for 3 days. To make sure the juice re-circulates through the eggs, turn the jars over in both the morning and evening. At the end of 3 days, your eggs are ready for use or be stored.

For storing eggs long term freezing is the way to go. You can go as is if you like juicy eggs. For this method just place the jar in the freezer. For the best all-around egg you should use the drain and freeze method. If you want a tough long lasting egg drain and dry your eggs until they are tacky and then freeze them. Once frozen the eggs will last a year or more.

Fishing the roe from a boat or the bank is simple as long as you remember one thing. The roe needs to be fished near, but not on the bottom. From a boat you can either drift or anchor and mooch the roe 6 to 18 inches from the bottom. Using a reel loaded with 8 pound test line and a 6 pound fluorocarbon leader, pin the roe on a No. 8 hook and employ a single split shot to get the bait down.

When fishing from the bank, the same rig can be used, but you'll need to employ a slip bobber rig to get the bait into the strike zone.

Chapter Twenty Four: Stream Trout Excitement!

I was about 10 years old. In my hand I held a willow switch with a half dozen rainbows and browns hanging from its length. Mom and I were sneaking along the banks of the Feather River a few miles from Quincy, California. We were taking turns fishing from the holes in the streamside brush that anglers had hollowed out over the years. The trout were feeding on cased caddis worms and they had a real fondness for the black and yellow Panther Martin spinner knotted to the end of our spinning rod's line.

Both my mom and dad are crackerjack stream trout anglers and I learned a great deal about effective stream trout tactics from them back in those days. On the afternoon my mom and I spent fishing the Feather more than 30 years ago I learned the importance of keeping my feet quiet and staying low. All the trout I caught were on the small side, but mom's were quite a bit bigger.

"You stay back and watch how I sneak up on this spot," she told me as we approached a pocket in the brush. Stopping on the trail I watched as mom crouched down and softly walk up just close enough to the opening to get the rod tip out over the water. Making a short underhand pitch she shot the spinner out into the current and closed the reel's bail.

Almost instantly the line came tight and the lure swung across the current and came to a stop next to the undercut bank below mom's position. Just as she started to turn the reel handle an unseen trout that had been lurking among the roots under the bank rocketed forward, grabbed the spinner and then darted back into its lair.

The light fiberglass rod bent nearly double. Looking back on the scene today, I'm surprised the line didn't hang up on a root. Keeping her cool, mom put the rod tip in the water and slowly used the reel to coax the trout in her direction.

After what seemed like an eternity the thick bodied trout boiled to the surface at mom's feet and she deftly slid it onto the bank where I pounced on it. Up until that time the holdover rainbow was the largest trout I'd ever seen, measuring 16 inches in length and weighing in at about two pounds. I remember being super excited and hoping that someday I could land a big 'ol trout like mom's!

Targeting stream trout is the quintessential trout fishing experience. Sure, in general, trout found in reservoirs and lakes average larger than stream trout, but fishing for stream trout reduces the sport of trout fishing to its basic elements. There are no sonar units, downriggers high powered boats or extensive tackle assortments to depend on. Stream fishing pits the angler against the trout. It's largely this chess game like quality that makes stream fishing so exciting and satisfying.

As with other forms of trout fishing, having the proper tackle is a crucial component of stream fishing success, second only in importance to employing proven tried and true tactics. The spinning rod and reel combination used for stream fishing is a lot like the outfit used for bank fishing at lakes, except the stream combo is lighter and nimbler.

Some experts recommend using a short spinning rod in the 5 to 6 foot range, reasoning that a short compact rod is easier to carry when maneuvering through streamside willows and brush. I won't argue that a short rod is easy to carry, but what is the purpose of a fishing rod? To catch fish, right? Well do you want a rod that is easy to carry or do you want the most effective rod for catching fish? If you're like me you want the most effective tool for hooking trout and that's why I use a 7 foot rod for stream fishing most of the time.

My pet stream fishing rod is a 7 foot Fenwick spinning rod that was presented to me by the Roostertails Fishing Club in Auburn, California after a public speaking engagement. This stick is rated for 4 to 10 pound line. It is a moderately fast action rod with plenty of flexibility in the upper third and solid backbone in the lower two thirds. Since my Fenwick boasts quality graphite construction, it provides superb sensitivity. I've matched the rod with a compact Abu Garcia spinning reel that holds 140 yards of 4 pound test line.

I spool the reel with 4 pound P-Line fluorocarbon line, further enhancing the rig's sensitivity and responsiveness. For all practical purposes fluorocarbon is invisible to fish, which is important in the gin clear waters of a trout stream. In addition it stretches very little and sinks readily. It is fluorocarbon's low stretch characteristics that make it more sensitive and responsive than standard monofilament.

Over the years, I've experimented with several different line weights. I've employed 2 pound test on the light end of the spectrum and 6, 8 and 10 pound test on the heavy end. I've settled on 4 pound test because it provides ample power for most stream applications. It is fine in diameter, yet it has enough body to keep it manageable and relatively tangle free.

Line capacity isn't a huge issue for the stream angler, but a silky smooth drag is. The dominant factor in any stream is current and current greatly magnifies the power and speed of even modest sized trout. If you are spooled up with 4 or even 6 pound line and hook a decent size trout that dives into a strong current be prepared to say goodbye if your drag hesitates or grabs.

Beyond a quality rod and reel, stream fishing requires a small well thought out array of terminal tackle. Tackle boxes are a pain to carry on a stream, so you'll want to carry your gear in a fishing vest or creel. This way your gear will be readily accessible.

Depth control is crucial when fishing for stream trout. In most situations you want your offering drifting near the bottom at the same speed as the current. Since stream depths and current velocities change constantly you'll need a variety of different sizes of split shot, so you can mix and match to achieve the proper depth and drift. Since the amount of weigh will need to be changed frequently, it is important to use removable split shot.

Lead split shot with squeezable tabs at the rear are cheap and easily removed, but the tabs make them more prone to snagging. Super soft English split shot that is composed of a combination of lead and tin doesn't have tabs, but due to its softness it is easily opened with your thumbnail.

English shot is significantly more expensive than standard lead shot, but it doesn't hang up as often. All things considered I prefer the English shot when I can get it. Generally you have to visit a fly shop to find it or you can order it directly from merry 'ol England via the Internet.

Along with split shot it is a good idea to carry a few eighth to quarter ounce bullet weights. You won't use these very often, but they are good to have just in case you are confronted with extra deep or extra fast water, conditions you're most likely to find in the early spring.

Targeting stream trout means fishing a variety of small baits and that means the aspiring stream angler will need a selection of small hooks. Octopus hooks in sizes 10 and 12 along with bait holders in sizes 8 and 10 will meet all the challenges that you'll face on the stream. Sharp strong hooks constructed of fine wire are important, so it isn't wise to skimp on quality to save money. Gamakatsu hooks are always my first choice. If they are not available Eagle Claw Lazer Sharps will get the job done.

Beyond split shot and hooks, I recommend carrying a Spartan assortment of wet flies and lures. Subsurface flies can be fished very effectively using spinning tackle in both lakes and streams.

In terms of lures you want to have both spoons and spinners. Every avid stream angler has his or her favorite lures. It isn't necessary to have a big selection of lures. More important is having confidence in the lures you use.

My all-time favorite spoon for stream fishing is an eighth or quarter ounce Kastmaster. I carry these in both gold and silver with gold being my first choice in most situations. In lakes I don't use traditional spinners very much, but in streams I can often be found working a spinner. I'm very particular about the type of spinner I use. For me there are Panther Martin spinners and then there are all the others.

I've been busting browns and rainbows on Panther Martins for more than 30 years and I have a tremendous level of confidence when I've got one on my line. I carry Panther Martins in the sixteenth, eighth and quarter ounce sizes. The best color scheme is black blade and body with yellow or red dots. For situations when I want more flash I go with a model featuring a gold blade.

Some anglers believe that you need lures in a wide range of different colors, but I disagree. When a stream trout hits a lure it is a reaction bite triggered in large part by the vibration and silhouette of the spoon or spinner. I believe the color of the lure is pretty far down on the list of importance in terms of whether or not a trout chooses to strike.

I avoid bright unnatural colors. My thought is that the metallic flash put off by a gold and silver lures mimics the flash of a baitfish, while the dark color scheme of my favorite Panther Martin is similar to the color of the nymphs that trout are accustomed to eating.

The spin angler can take plenty of trout on flies and lures, but artificials can't compete with the effectiveness of natural baits. Stream trout are opportunists by nature and will take a wide range of natural baits, in fact any small organism found in the stream or that falls in the stream might just find itself residing inside a trout.

Having said that, I employ four different natural baits when targeting stream trout. Worms are my favorite. The baby night crawlers found at tackle shops are great, but smaller "garden worms" that I dig myself are even better. I've tried red worms and while they will catch trout I'm not a big fan of them. They are too small and too fragile for most applications.

Depending on the size of the worms I'm using, I pin them on either a No. 8 or 10 bait holder hook. A lot of anglers make the mistake of balling their worm up on the hook. This results in a lifeless worm glob. A better strategy is to lightly pin the worm on the hook. This way as it drifts along it is able to move and wriggle, resulting in a much more natural looking presentation and correspondingly more hookups.

Running a close second to worms in my stream trout arsenal are crickets. Trout love crickets and grasshoppers, so they are a wonderful choice. The crickets I buy generally come 50 at a time in a brown tub with a chunk of potato in it for the crickets to feed on. The lids on these tubs come off pretty easily. I only had to lose all my crickets once to realize that I needed a better way of carrying them on the stream.

Fortunately for us there are commercially manufactured cricket cages available on the market. These cages have a screw on lid at the top, a metal or plastic mesh middle section and a tapered funnel shaped opening on the bottom that is plugged with a cork. When you pull out the cork there is enough room for a single cricket to exit the cage and on the hook he goes!

Crickets are pretty active and transitioning them from the tub into a cricket cage can be tough, but there is a trick you can use to make things easier. Crickets are cold blooded. If you pop the tub of them into a freezer or ice chest for a short time they will become lethargic, making it a simple task to make the transfer. When you expose crickets to the cold you want to keep an eye on them. You don't want them to die. You just want to slow them down.

If you choose to take the time to catch grasshoppers they are even more effective than crickets and you can keep them in the same cage you'd keep crickets in. To catch grasshoppers you'll need some sort of fine meshed net with a long handle. With net in hand, head out to a grassy, brushy area and let the hunt begin. Heck if you've got the time, catching 'hoppers can be almost as fun as stalking trout!

Crickets and grasshopper are placed on the hook in the same way. The hook point is inserted into the chest just below the head and exits the body where the abdomen connects to the rear of the chest. To keep them securely in place, push the eye of the hook into the chest. A No. 10 bait holder hook is about right for crickets while a larger No. 8 bait holder works better for grasshoppers.

Trout, especially rainbows, seem to be genetically wired to eat salmon eggs, since both hatchery trout and wild trout living in streams that don't have a salmon run will readily gobble up salmon eggs, despite the fact that they have never seen one before. The first trout I ever caught came on a salmon egg and I've caught countless others on eggs over the years.

There are a few different brands of salmon eggs on the market. The best I've ever used come from the Pautzke Bait Company in Washington State. Pautzke's Green Label eggs are the stuff of legend on most West Coast trout streams, likely having produced more trout than all other baits combined.

When most anglers think of salmon eggs they envision bright red eggs. Red eggs work great, but for a subtler presentation I like to have some yellow, orange or natural colored eggs on hand too. Eggs are best fished one or two at a time. I fish my eggs with a No. 12 octopus hook imbedded in them. If I'm using two eggs I pin the hook through the first egg and slide the egg up onto the leader. The second egg has the hook imbedded in it and the second egg is slid down against it.

The final bait I'll discuss in the lowly mealworm. Mealies are a light colored larval worm that are about 1 inch long. They are plump, juicy and helpless, making them a prime target for a hungry trout. I like to place them on a No. 10 bait holder hook. I thread them onto the hook such that the entire shank of the hook and the eye is concealed in the worm and only the bend and the point are exposed.

Rods, reels, tackle and baits, that is half the picture for the successful stream trout angler. The second half of the picture is tactics and techniques. When fishing from a boat your sonar unit often locates the fish. The stream angler doesn't have any nifty technological short cuts for locating fish. Instead, they use their eyes and knowledge of trout behavior to find their quarry. This skill is known as "reading the stream".

Looking at a stream you will notice that depths and current speeds are constantly changing. Stream trout have two primary considerations. The first is security and the second is food. Stream trout don't like to feel exposed and they will always hold near a feature such as strong current, deep water, a fallen tree or an undercut bank that can provide them with protection at a moment's notice, should a bank side predator or a bird of prey show up on the scene.

We all know the basics of budgeting our money. If you don't have more money coming in than is going out you will eventually go broke. Well, trout have to budget their calories in much the same way. They've got to consume more calories than they burn or starvation will result. This being the case trout like to sit in areas that feature a break in the current, allowing them to hold and expend minimal energy while having immediate access to prey items being swept along by the current.

An example of a classic holding area is the pocket of slack water that exists on the downstream side of rocks and boulders. In the pocket there is very little current, but immediately to the left, right and above the current is scooting along briskly. A trout holding in such a location is equivalent to us setting in an easy chair with conveyer belts dotted with tasty snacks surrounding us on three sides. Other examples of prime current breaks include fallen trees, sudden drop offs, shelves, bends in the current and root tangled undercut banks.

There is no substitute for on the water experience when it comes to reading a stream. Success and failure are both great instructors. When you catch a trout make a mental note of the type of area it was holding in. When you blow it and see trout spook and bolt for cover. Think about where they were located and how you might approach such locations with more stealth in the future.

Speaking of stealth and approaching trout, when you're on the stream try to have a hunter's mindset. By a hunter's mindset I'm referring to approaching stream fishing with the idea of stalking the trout and remaining unseen and unheard as much as possible. To remain unseen stay low and keep to the shadows as much as possible. Try never to have the sun at your back. Stream trout expect danger to come from above and if they see your shadow they will bolt thinking there is a threat coming from above them.

Water is a great conductor of vibrations and in the thin water of a trout stream vibrations can spook fish, particularly the large wild and holdover trout we all dream of hooking. As you move along the stream don't rush and be sure to walk softly this will keep the vibrations you create to a minimum.

Most of the time you will have no problem approaching trout effectively from the bank, but on streams that are lined with thick brush it is advantageous at times to get into the water. If the weather is warm put on a pair of old shoes and some shorts and you're in business. At other times you'll want to don a pair of hip waders. Leave the chest waders to the fly guys. In the vast majority of situations it is never necessary for the spin angler to venture into water that is much beyond knee deep.

The culminating event for the stream angler is the presentation. In general terms, stream trout do most of their feeding near the bottom and are accustomed to encountering prey that is drifting helplessly along at the same speed as the current. When using bait you want your offering dead drifting near the bottom at the same rate as the surrounding water. When the bait moves slower or faster than the surrounding current drag results and this will greatly reduce the chances of getting a hit.

With all this in mind the bait angler moves upstream against the current, making short casts angled up current. The amount of weight pinched on the line from 14 to 20 inches above the bait is constantly altered so that the bait drifts naturally along the bottom regardless of the depth and current's velocity. It is better to start out too light and add weight than to start out heavily and drag the bait unnaturally through a pocket of holding water.

The first cast to a potential hold is made upstream of it and the bait is allowed to drift down to the trout. You want to drift the bait on both sides of the pocket a couple times and finally before moving on to another spot drop the bait directly into the pocket's slack water and let it set there for a several seconds.

Since you'll be casting up current, slack is going to develop in the line as the bait drifts back toward you. It is important to limit the amount of slack that forms since it will rob your ability to feel the bite and will result in more frequent snags.

A skilled stream angler keeps the line between the rod and a drifting bait nearly tight, walking the bait along like a dog on a leash. With a short cast the slack can be picked up by simply raising the tip of the rod. That is one of the reasons I like a long rod. In situations where a longer cast is need, the rod tip should still be raised, but the reel will need to be used to pick up extra slack.

Since current velocities vary a great deal across a stream it is important to keep a high rod tip as this will keep as much line as possible off the water. If your bait is drifting with a moderately fast current and the line is lying in a fast current, the fast current will catch the slack and pull the bait along unnaturally.

So how do you identify a bite? At times a trout will dart out, grab the bait and shoot back where it came from. This type of bite is obvious, since it results in a hard tug and the trout generally hooks itself.

At other times a trout will inhale the bait and then drift along with the current. With this type of bite you feel a small sharp tap or two. Wait a beat or two before lifting the tip and loading the rod and the trout will be hooked. If your rod tip is already held high, set the hook by cranking the reel several times.

The third common type of bite comes when the trout inhales the bait and doesn't move at all. This type of bite is signaled by the line stopping dead in the water as if the bait is hung on the bottom. If your line stops, it could be a snag or it could be a trout, but you've got to assume that it's a fish. As a result when the line stops give the rod tip a short sharp tug. If the sinker is hung up this will often jar it loose, if there is a trout mouthing the bait it's Fish On!

The strategy for fishing with nymphs is much the same as when fishing bait, except rather than retrieving the bait and casting again when the rig drifts back to your position as is the case with natural baits, I like to allow a nymph or wet fly to continue drifting downstream until it reaches the end of the line. Even then I allow it to hang in the current for a few seconds as I jig it a bit. Trout will seldom hit a natural bait when held in the current in this way, but they will often hammer a wet fly.

Lure fishing requires a significantly different strategy than fishing with bait or flies. Instead of moving upstream, the lure angler is most effective traveling downstream. It doesn't matter if you are fishing a spoon or spinner the basic presentation with a lure is to cast straight across the stream and allow the lure to swing across the current on a tight line. You rarely need to work the reel, because the current plunging past the lure will give it action. Once the lure has swung directly downstream of your position, let it hang in the current for a few moments before retrieving it slowly along the bank. Strikes can come at any time during this process.

Lures don't need to be fished as close to the bottom as baits or wet flies, but you don't want them skimming along the surface either. If the current is such that your spoon or spinner isn't digging deep enough, add enough split shot above the leader to get it to the desired depth. In general, I like my lures to run about two thirds of the way to the bottom. For example if the water is three feet deep, I want my lure running a foot off the bottom.

In closing I've got a couple final thoughts to pass on in relation to stream fishing. First of all most stream anglers with the exception of fly guys don't carry a net. While I often don't carry one either, it is a good idea to have one on hand. You can take care of most fish nicely without a net, but when you catch that brown trout of a lifetime you'll be glad to have a net hanging from your belt.

Finally, as you traverse your favorite trout streams, be sure not to leave any litter behind in the form of discarded line or empty bait containers. It is bad enough to see this type of junk dotting the shoreline of a man made reservoir, but it is a real shame when trash ruins the ambience of a babbling trout stream. I carry a large zip lock bag with me on the stream to carry out some of the trash that other folks leave and you should do the same. It's a way of giving something back to the fishery!

Chapter Twenty Five: Egging On Trout

Trout and salmon eggs, salmon eggs and trout, they go together like cookies and milk or baseball and hotdogs. Trout have been gobbling eggs for eons and trout anglers have been using salmon eggs to catch trout for a century, perhaps longer.

We all have our favorite trout baits and lures and truth be told most traditional lures, baits and flies will catch trout some of the time, yet it always pays to utilize the most effective tool available. From a bait fishing standpoint it's hard to come up with a more versatile and effective bait for both lake and stream fishing then salmon eggs. Here's why....

Both planted trout and more importantly holdover and wild trout relish salmon eggs. Now it's easy to understand why the wild rainbows residing in the Sacramento River eat eggs, after all they are surrounded by spawning salmon for several months of the year, but what about the planter that has never seen anything to eat beyond government issue trout pellets. Why does that rainbow go out of its way to inhale that bright red Green Label egg?

I think on an instinctive level the goal of the fish is twofold. First a trout or salmon is motivated to destroy any spawn it encounters such that its own offspring will have a better chance at survival. Second eggs are packed with nutrition and the trout seem to know that a loose egg or two is not a meal that should be passed up.

Regardless of why trout hit them, eggs are an outstanding tool for trout whether your goal is a limit of fryers for breakfast or hooking a reclusive brown that has survived many trout seasons.

Let's look at some methods for using salmon eggs and explore the various salmon eggs available to match a range of different situations.

Some folks look at egg fishing as the method of choice for the unsophisticated angler in search of planters. While fooling trout with eggs may not be as tough as catching bone fish on the Christmas Island flats, the aspiring egg angler will still benefit from having top notch gear tailored to the task at hand.

For lake fishing where vegetation isn't a factor you'll want a 7 to 8 foot medium action-spinning rod. The soft action rod will allow you to cast long distances with minimal weight without flinging your soft eggs off the hook.

For stream fishing a 6 to 7 foot fast action rod is in order. The faster action gives you the power you need to control fish in current, while the shorter length makes navigating streamside brush easier.

Both rods should be balanced with a spinning reel spooled with standard 4 or 6 lb. copolymer line like Trilene or P-Line CXX. I like moss colored line, as I believe the fish have a tough time seeing it.

Some folks may be tempted to spool up with fluorocarbon. That's not a good idea. I advocated using fluorocarbon leaders. However fluorocarbon line sinks and some of the egg fishing techniques I'll describe work best with neutral buoyancy copolymer line that stays near the surface of the water.

With your rod and reel taken care of we'll need some components and other toys. Start off with a couple spools of fluorocarbon leader material in 4 and 6 pound test. Next add to that a selection of octopus hooks in size 8, 10 and 12. I mostly go with either red or black Eagle Claw Lazer Sharps.

You'll also need a selection of small black swivels, split shot and some ¼ ounce bullet weights.

To round out your gear selection you might have to shop around a bit to find exactly what is needed. First you'll want to find a P-Line Trout Fishing Bead Assortment. The box contains 6mm and 8mm beads in 20 different colors. Next you'll want some steelhead fishing yarn in subtle orange, yellow and pink hues. You don't want the really bright stuff in most circumstances.

The final piece of the puzzle is an assortment of standard slip bobbers as well as an assortment of small ½ and 5/8 inch foam strike indicators that are used by fly anglers.

Let's take a moment to talk about the eggs themselves. There are all sorts of salmon eggs on the market. For quality, selection and cost Pautzke eggs can't be beat. They've been selling their "industry standard" Green Label eggs since the 1930's.

It's the aforementioned green and white lidded jar of red Green Label eggs many of us started trout fishing with and it's these eggs we think of when we think of fishing salmon eggs for trout. Yet there is far more to the Pautzke egg line up than the tried and true Green Labels. I think there are at least two other "models" of egg that every serious trout angler should be carrying for both lake and stream fishing.

If you check out the Pautzke website you'll find that they produce six different types of bottled egg in the Ball's O' Fire line. I'm sorry but I seldom run Green Labels anymore instead when I want a red egg I usually go with a Premium Egg. Hand-picked from late harvest king salmon, Premium is the highest quality egg in the Balls O' Fire line. These top of the line eggs are uniform in size, tightly graded, clean and big eggs. There are no loose fragments of eggs in the jar. They are the highest quality egg available. Where you might use two or three green label eggs to cover a hook you'll only need one Premium egg to do the same job.

As good as red eggs can be, when it's time to fool holdover rainbows and big wild browns with spawning on the brain, natural colored eggs are best. This brings us to Pautzke's yellow and orange eggs. They call their orange eggs, "Orange Deluxe" and the yellow ones are dubbed "Yellow Jackets".

Orange Deluxe salmon eggs aid anglers in presenting a more natural colored salmon egg to salmon, trout and steelhead. For the most part, natural color eggs aren't red, rather a shade of orange. Orange Deluxe eggs are carefully cooked to emulate the natural tint that salmon, trout and steelhead eggs have.

Yellow Jackets are similar to Orange Deluxe salmon eggs as they strive to retain characteristics of natural colored eggs found in lakes, streams and reservoirs. Yellow Jackets carry a natural yellow tint to them.

If you check my gear I may or may not have other eggs with me, but I always have Premium red, Orange Deluxe and Yellow Jackets. If I had to pick one as being my favorite it would be the Orange Deluxe simply because it is such a versatile natural looking egg.

You could probably write an entire book on ways you can rig and fish salmon eggs. I'm going to move quickly and outline a few of my favorite methods.

Let's start with stream fishing. In the fall the absolute best stream fishing opportunities exist where streams enter lakes that hold brown trout. You've got to check your regulations because on some lakes these areas are closed to fishing. Once you locate a brown trout lake that allows you to fish near the inlet, it's time to explore both the stream side and lake side of the inlet.

Browns spawn in the fall and winter. It's very common for these fish to stack up both in the lake offshore of inflowing tributaries and in the lower reaches of the tributaries themselves. Holdover rainbows move in and patrol these same areas looking for loose brown trout spawn.

A natural presentation is always important, but it is absolutely key when dealing with wary trout holding in shallow water. There are two ways to target these trout. You can either drift a natural colored egg along the bottom or drift one suspended beneath a small bobber.

For drifting near the bottom. Take your main line and tip it with a swivel. To the swivel attach 16 inches of fluorocarbon leader and tip the leader with a No. 12 hook. If the current is light additional weight won't be needed. Simply bait the hook with two eggs and you're ready to fish. If there is a good deal of current you'll need to add small split shot above the swivel until you get enough weight on to keep the egg near the bottom, but moving at the same pace as the current.

When presenting eggs on this rig you want to cast up and across stream and let the eggs drift back down toward your position as realistically as possible. You'll need to manage your line. You want the eggs drifting with the current, but you can't allow a bunch of slack to develop.

Sometimes a strike will be felt as a tap, but at other times nothing will be felt and the only clue will be the line stopping or twitching. If anything odd happens set the hook. Hook sets are free and you'll be surprised how often what you thought was a rock turns out to be a trout. When fishing eggs guys that watch the line typically catch more trout than guys that rely on "feel" to detect bites.

To fish the same areas using a float you set up your rod the same way, except your apply a fly fishing float to the line above the swivel. How deep you believe the fish to be holding dictates where you place the bobber on the line. It's best not to use any additional weight if possible, but at times when the water is deep and/or moving fast a larger bobber and a few split shot will be needed to get your eggs in the strike zone.

The presentation with the bobber is up and across stream just like with the bottom drifting rig. The only real difference is that you're looking at the bobber to tell you when a strike is happening. You still have to use good line management and remember when that bobber goes down you must reel until you feel the fish and then set the hook. If you fail to do this you'll miss trout due to slack in your line.

These two methods are not used just for targeting browns. I fish eggs for planted rainbows and brook trout the exact same ways. The key is presenting the egg with a stealthy natural drift.

For lake fishing situations I use the same basic rigs. My favorite method is using as slip bobber set up such that the eggs drift just off the bottom. In streams I almost always use orange or yellow eggs. In the lake I use all the colors and often pair them to create combinations.

If a slip bobber isn't working or I'm too lazy to set one up, I'll often set up a bottom drifting rig with no weight and bait the hook with a couple eggs. I then cast the eggs out as far as I can and let them settle to the bottom. Every 15 seconds or so, I move the eggs a few inches. The movement catches the attention of the trout. When they come in to investigate they often munch the eggs.

Don't worry about casting too far offshore when lake fishing in the fall, winter and spring. Remember that when the water is cool the baitfish often gravitate to the bank and the trout follow them. In the early winter at lakes like New Melones it's not uncommon to hook quality trout within a rod length of the bank.

Mike Bogue of Mike Bogue's Guide Service is one of the state's top guides when it comes to catching salmon, trout and steelhead in the Sacramento River between Redding and Red Bluff. Mike has come up with the exciting hybrid egg combos that he uses for tempting big trout in moving water.

The trout fishing on the Sacramento can be downright phenomenal for wild rainbows. The trout feed heavily on salmon roe, so it makes sense that Bogue would develop some unique methods of fishing eggs to meet the demands of the Sac's deep fast flowing water.

"**There are many ways** to imitate salmon eggs tumbling down the Sacramento River. Glo Bugs and yarn flies are two of my favorites," confides Bogue. "However, my top bait is a Glo Bug with a Pautzke Orange Deluxe salmon egg on the hook. This gives you the salmon egg look and the smell of the real thing. There's no bait better than a real salmon egg on your line. "

"**To rig this I use a** slinky for weight, 6 pound P-Line fluorocarbon leader and a Glo Bug. I'll cast the bugs below riffles where salmon are spawning or have spawned. In addition to trout, this setup works well for steelhead in low clear conditions or when you are out of roe. I also use it under a float. For steelhead, I use 10 pound P-Line fluorocarbon leader, 12 – 15 pound P-line mainline and an Eagle Claw No. 4 Lazar Sharp Hook in the egg loop. It's best to tie in a No. 12 Corky with your favorite color yarn. In addition, when using this setup with a float I put a bead in the egg loop," tips Bogue.

"**This method is bound** to catch bows and steelies, but if you aren't getting bit feel free to alter the color combination. It's ok to switch out other Corky's (beads), yarn combinations and also substitute Yellow Jackets, Orange Deluxe (my favorite) or Premium salmon eggs," Bogue concluded.

Chapter Twenty Six: Worms...The Must Have Bait

Worms are low down and dirty. After all, they spend their lives crawling around in dirt or worse...manure! However worms do have a positive side, namely their value as top notch fishing bait. Bass, trout, panfish, catfish and even bright fresh from the sea steelhead have a soft spot for fat juicy worms.

Traditionally speaking, when it comes to using worms for bait, worms and trout fishing go together like fried chicken and potato salad on the 4th of July! Yet it seems like every year I encounter fewer and fewer trout anglers employing worms. The vast majority of trout targeting boaters I meet troll with lures and plugs exclusively, while most shore anglers I come across spend nearly all of their time soaking floating dough baits.

Has the current generation of trout anglers come to the conclusion that their modern sexy offerings outdistance the effectiveness of their grandfathers' night crawlers or have the advertising campaigns of tackle and trout bait companies simply overshadowed the effectiveness of the low crawling worm?

I tend to believe that most of the trout anglers entering the sport these days simply overlook worms, because they don't truly grasp how effective they can be. Let's face it you'll never meet a night crawler being represented by an advertising agency!

For the uninitiated anglers out there, I'm going to share a dirty little secret with you. Not only are worms one of the most effective trout baits available, but are also among the simplest to employ effectively whether you are firmly seated on the bank or trolling from the stern of a high tech aluminum trout sled.

Let's kick things off by exploring the art of trout worming from the bank of a lake or reservoir, before looking at how trollers can employ worms.

For the still water bank angler there are really two ways to present a worm, either off the bottom or suspending beneath the water's surface. Most of the time, trout can be found feeding and holding near the bottom, so that's were you should present your bait most of the time.

The key here is presenting your bait NEAR the bottom, not ON the bottom. This is why PowerBait and other trout dough concoctions float. When teamed with a sliding sinker rig and a 1 to 3 foot leader these baits float up off the bottom right into the cruising zone of the trout.

Taking a cue from your dough soaking brothers, you'll want to float your worm off the bottom too. This can be accomplished by teaming your worm with a marshmallow or injecting your worm with air using a worm blower or hypodermic needle. In most cases I prefer to float my worms with an injection of air, because this makes for a more natural looking offering.

I firmly believe that a worm gives me two distinct advantages over dough baits. First of all, experience has demonstrated that worms provide me with the best shot at hooking holdovers and wild trout such as the elusive brown trout that call many of our lakes and reservoirs home simply because worms represent a "natural" bait. A worm is "real" meat and the trout know it.

Secondly unlike dough baits, worms appeal to all of a trout senses. Dough baits put out lots of scent, but their visual attractiveness is limited to an array of bright colors. Worms take things a step farther. Like dough baits worms put off scent, but they also offer eye-catching movement as they wriggle and undulate. These subtle movements can be the difference between a hookup and a rejection, especially when the trout concerned in an experienced holdover or wild fish.

In situations when I have reason to believe that the trout in a given lake are suspended, I clip off my sliding sinker rigs and replace them with a slip bobber rigs. A slip bobber allows me to cast my worm a good distance offshore and fish it at a set depth anywhere from 5 to 30 or more feet deep. In this situation, I don't inject my worm with air, since I don't want it floating up. I just want it to hang wiggling in the water column.

If trout hit a bank angler's worm because it looks natural, I can't explain why a trout would hit a trolled worm, because a worm presented in such a way looks anything but natural. Yet many times trout will grab a trolled worm with vigor while ignoring all other offerings.

When the Styrofoam worm container comes out during a trout trolling adventure on my boat, it's because the fishing is tough and artificials are not producing well. In that situation, I sometimes run a straight "naked" crawler without adding a dodger or string of flashers.

Trolling naked worms is the picture of simplicity. I take my main line and attach it to a high quality trolling swivel. To the other end of the swivel I connect a 24 to 36 inch 6 lb. fluorocarbon leader tipped with a No. 6 Owner Mosquito hook. Using a worm threader, I slide a whole night crawler up over the hook and onto the leader. I thread the worm on the threader such that about a 1/2 inch of worm dangles behind the hook. Rigged this way the worm will rotate when trolled through the water.

If the trout are near the surface, I add a couple slit shot above the swivel and topline the worm from 200 to 250 feet behind the boat while keeping the speed from . 5 to 1 mph. If the trout are suspended I run the same rig minus the split shot 100 to 150 feet behind a downrigger weight.

My stealthily trolled worms have produced a lot of trout for me over the years, but other anglers do equally as well when they run a threaded worm behind dodgers or flashers. These guys are typically the old timers that grew up pulling worms behind blades. With blade set ups the areas for experimentation are whether you employ a whole crawler or only a portion of the crawler and how far you put the threaded bait behind the blades. Sometimes the trout will prefer a worm crowded tight to the rear of the blades. At other times they want a worm trailing as far as 6 feet behind the blades.

A Ford Fender teamed with a night crawler was the favorite trolling combination of our grandfathers because it produced trout and it will still produce trout today. Today's trout angler may have gone high tech, but the trout haven't changed.

This being the case, remember that when your high tech lures and laboratory created dough baits fail, you can look to the lowly worm to save the day.

Worms.... Trout anglers should never leave home without them!

Chapter Twenty Seven: Teaming Flies With Conventional Gear

Conventional tackle trout anglers that have never used a fly rod, very often view fly fishing as a complicated aristocratic approach to catching trout that is difficult to learn and painfully expensive.

While there is a small percentage of the fly fishing fraternity that do look at conventional anglers with a jaundiced eye, most fly guys are just like us. They are anglers that crave the excitement that comes from hooking hard fighting trout!

I've spent a lot of time over the years with a fly rod in my hand and I've enjoyed every minute of it. At its core, I've never found the sport of fly fishing to be complicated, but it is certainly possible to make it that way. As far as being expensive, I believe that was true in the past, but when you look at the cost of a sonar unit, a set of downriggers, quality rods and a set of lures, dodgers and flashers it's really hard to point a finger at the fly fishing aficionados and accuse them of engaging in a sport that is any more expensive than ours.

For me, using fly tackle has never been an aesthetic endeavor. I always try to employ the technique that will allow me to hook more and bigger trout in any given situation. Back in my teenage years I learned that flies would often draw strikes from spooky heavily pressured trout that looked at lures and baits with complete indifference. Yet, much to my chagrin, I also determined that there are many situations when presenting a fly with traditional fly tackle can be difficult or downright impossible. Shorelines that feature a lot of vegetation, deep briskly flowing water and trout holding in deepwater represent a few of the situations where presenting a fly with traditional fly tackle can be very difficult at best.

Luckily for us, flies work great when teamed with conventional tackle. My dad was the one that turned me on to fishing flies on spinning tackle back in 1990. Dad and I were fishing the Cassel section of Hat Creek, near Burney, California. Hat Creek flows into Cassel as a big meandering brook, before being necked down into a deep fast flowing hydroelectric canal. There are a lot of trout that hold along the bottom of the canal. After we failed to hook up with our fly tackle in the slow flowing section of the creek, we turned our attention to the canal.

Trying to work the bottom of the canal with fly tackle is pretty tough. Generally bait and lure anglers do well in the canal, so dad and I broke out our spinning rods and went to work with bait. Since we were fishing just after the Fourth of July holiday, the canal had been subjected to intense pressure. After an hour of fishing with only one small rainbow to show for our effort, I was ready to go check out another stretch of stream. Dad on the other hand was determined to hook the trout we could occasionally see sulking along the bottom.

"I wonder if they will hit a fly," my dad asked. "Probably, but you'll never get a fly down to them," I told him. "I can with this spinning rod," came his reply. Full of skepticism, I watched dad knot a small shrimp imitating nymph to the end of his line and then pinch on a string of split shot about two feet above it.

Shooting a cast up stream to the far side of the canal, dad allowed the rig to sink and roll along the bottom. Once the rig reached his position, dad engaged the reel. Presently, the line tightened and the fly started to rise and swing back toward our bank. Seconds later the line tightened as a husky rainbow inhaled the fly.

Dad had his hands full fighting both the fish and the current, but a couple minutes later the trout was struggling inside his net. I might have set some sort of speed record rigging up my spinning rod with a fly, but I didn't complete the job before dad had hooked his second trout. For the rest of the afternoon we hammered trout after trout. By dinnertime we'd landed and released more than 40 rainbows!

That day opened up a whole new world for me. Since then teaming flies with both spinning and trolling gear has been an important element in my trout fishing bag of tricks. Over the years, I've come to recognize that the most effective approach is often the simplest, regardless of the species being pursued. Teaming flies with conventional gear when targeting trout is nothing if not simple. I believe this approach is effective, because it isn't often used and presents pressured trout with something that they haven't seen before.

Pressured and spooky trout need to feed just the same as trout that are perfectly relaxed, but when subjected to pressure they quickly begin to associate baits, lures and traditional presentations with danger. Since these trout haven't seen a slew of flies, they don't associate them with danger and are willing to take an exploratory swipe at them.

Most aquatic insects spend their time hiding among rocks, bottom debris and weeds. They live this way for one simple reason, they don't want to be eaten. When the time comes for insects like mayflies or caddis flies to swim to the surface in order to hatch into their adult form they become highly vulnerable to trout as they move through open water. Whether trolling with flies or casting them with spinning gear your goal is to mimic a helpless nymph, shrimp, leech or baitfish attempting to navigate open water. This means that a slow no frills presentation is the way to go most of the time.

Before we consider some different rigging options, let's take a moment to discuss which types of flies are best suited to being teamed with spinning or trolling gear. Traditional fly anglers use dry flies that represent insects resting on the surface of the water. They also use nymphs and wet flies that imitate immature forms of aquatic insects that live underwater. Finally, they also employ a class of larger flies called streamers that imitate minnows, leaches and other large prey items found below the surface of the water. When trout are feeding on the surface, traditional fly tackle is the best tool for catching them. For the conventional tackle angler, it is subsurface patterns that hold the most promise.

Fly anglers generally carry a substantial selection of flies to match the various hatches they encounter throughout the course of a season. I have never tried to match a specific insect hatch when using flies teamed with conventional tackle. I just employ impressionistic patterns that have the general appearance of forage items that trout feed on throughout the year. As a result, the conventional tackle angler only needs to carry a handful of different patterns in a few different sizes.

Over the years the woolly bugger has emerged as my favorite streamer pattern. If you only carry one fly pattern with you, this should be it. The woolly bugger, an updated version of the woolly worm, sports a chenille body that is covered with hackle and a marabou tail. Both the hackle and the marabou look extremely lifelike under the water, pulsing and writhing continually with the slightest movement. I carry both black and olive colored buggers with black being my favorite in sizes 6 and 10.

In addition to woolly buggers, you'll want a few size 6 marabou streamer flies in white, orange and black. A few No. 8

and 10 light and dark colored stonefly nymphs featuring soft hackle legs along with a couple size No. 12 or 14 soft hackle pheasant tails will round out your assortment nicely.

For teaming flies with spinning gear I use two basic rigging methods, a casting rig and a slip bobber/casting bubble rig. In this chapter I'll focus on the casting rig and I'll devote a complete chapter to fly/bobber tactics.

To set up a casting rig for general casting or drifting applications I tie a swivel to the end of my main line with 24 inches of 4 pound fluorocarbon leader attached to it. I tie my fly of choice to the end of the leader and add an appropriate amount of weight above the swivel in the form of split shot. If I need to go really heavy, I'll often put a quarter to half ounce bullet weight above the swivel.

In still water situations, whether fishing from the bank or a boat, I fish the casting rig by casting it out as far as possible and then retrieve it slowly. I usually start out with a steady retrieve, but if that doesn't work, I'll mix things up by imparting twitches and pauses.

Typically, I'll begin fishing right beneath the surface and then work progressively deeper by counting the rig down. I seldom use nymph patterns in still water since they have little built in action. Instead I stick with woolly buggers and marabou streamers, because the marabou they incorporate constantly moves in a very lifelike manner.

In rivers and streams I use my woolly buggers and marabou streamers a great deal, but I also make use of nymphs. At times I'll even tie two flies on a leader and fish them both at the same time. This is accomplished by tying one fly to the end of the casting rig's leader and then adding a 12 inch section of leader to the bend of the first fly's hook tipped with a second fly of equal or smaller size.

Moving water is most effectively covered by using a drift and swing presentation. To accomplish this, the rig is cast directly across the current or a bit upstream. Allow the rig to sink on a semi-tight line. When the line tightens below your position allow the fly to swing across the current and back to your side of the flow.

At this point don't be in a hurry to retrieve the rig. Instead allow it to hang in the current for several seconds as you slowly pump the rod tip. It always amazes me how many trout I pick up by jigging or pumping a fly right next to the bank on a tight line.

Having the correct amount of weight on your line is critical when fishing current. On one hand you want enough weight to get the rig to the bottom on the drift, but you don't want so much weight that the rig rolls through the rocks, constantly getting snagged. It is best to use several small split shot for weight. This allows you to add and remove weights until the rig is just ticking the bottom occasionally on the drift. As the rig is drifting, strikes can be very subtle. If the line stops or twitches, set the hook. Once the rig begins to swing the hits will be hard and the trout will generally hook itself on the strike.

For trolling applications streamer flies are most useful, but occasionally I employ a nymph or soft hackle fly too. If you really want to keep things simple you can rig up a rod with the casting rig we've already discussed, weight it with a quarter or half ounce bullet weight and put it out between 100 and 200 feet behind the boat.

Naturally, a woolly bugger or marabou streamer trolled in this manner will have minimal action. At times that is just what the doctor ordered. If a straight no frills approach isn't working try twitching the rod. This will cause the fly to act erratically, rising and falling as it comes through the water.

Some anglers swear by teaming a fly with a wiggle disk for slow trolling in lakes. A wiggle disk is simply a clear round piece of concave plastic that you put on the line directly above the fly. As the disk moves through the water it wiggles back and forth and that movement is transferred to the fly.

Sometimes I use Wiggle Disks, but at other times I employ small dodgers like Sep's Side Kicks and Strike Masters. Instead I prefer to team my flies with a small dodger. I've had some memorable action while trolling black or olive woolly buggers and marabous behind a watermelon colored Sep's Sidekick.

If I want to get a fly down a little below the surface, but don't want to use my downriggers I've found that tying the mainline from my rod to a deep diving crankbait and then running a 36 inch leader off the back of the plug tipped with a streamer or nymph can be a highly effective approach when the fishing turns tough. The plug takes the fly down 6 to 12 or more feet below the surface. The disturbance and flash put off by the crankbait attracts the trout and when they see the fly they grab it. I think this rig works because it is something they have never seen before and the trout hit it out of curiosity.

At this point teaming flies with conventional tackle remains in its infancy and few angles are doing it. Will this approach ever become wildly popular? I doubt it, but it does present anglers with a means of hooking highly pressured spooky trout. In this chapter I've only outlined the basics and explained how I use flies. I hope you'll incorporate flies into you trout fishing repertoire.

Remember in a lot of ways, this is a whole new approach, so you are only limited by your imagination. My buddy Jim English has had great success trolling a woolly bugger behind his boat without any added weight such that the fly drags across or just under the surface. That isn't something I would think of trying, but you certainly can't argue with success!

Chapter Twenty Eight: Trouting Weather Or Not

Bass anglers are acutely aware of the effects the weather has on the behavior and habits of bass. Because of the physiology of bass, the effects of weather changes can be profound. Trout anglers are nowhere near as in tune with the effects weather has on their quarry and with good reason. Trout don't react as strongly to weather changes as bass and a lot of other fish species, but they do react never the less.

A lot of the information I'm going to present in this chapter is anecdotal and based largely on my own observations, since there is very little research as to how trout react to weather and weather changes. Before we delve into a discussion of weather and trout behavior I'd like to encourage all the anglers reading this to begin keeping a fishing journal if this is something they aren't already doing.

The journal doesn't have to be in depth, so long as you record the conditions including the date, the weather, water temperature, methods employed, the level of success you experienced and anything you observed that seemed interesting or significant.

Over time you will begin to notice trends, giving you clues about how to approach fishing during certain seasons and how to deal with situations such as weather changes. Over the years my journal has become an invaluable tool in predicting when and how to catch fish of all kinds including trout.

So what are the worst possible weather related scenarios for the trout angler? That's a pretty easy question to answer, since there are only two situations that can make for really tough fishing. The first is an abrupt change in water temperature and the second is fishing immediately after a low pressure area passes.

When the water temperature changes quickly it severely affects the metabolism of trout and other fish because they are cold blooded. The worst temperature changes are those that lower the temperature even if the temperature remains within the comfort zone of the trout. An example of this would be a cold snap that occurs during the fall or spring.

Let's say the rainbows are up in the shallows of a lake or reservoir because the water temperature is 59 degrees and then the surface temperature suddenly is driven down to 56 degrees. Now we are only talking about a 3 degree drop and the whole time the temperature has remained in the comfort zone of rainbow trout, but the trout will inevitable become sluggish with the change. Being cold blooded such a change immediately causes the metabolism of the trout to slow down and they will feel less energetic. This means that they will feed less and be less likely to chase moving offerings such as trolled lures until they become acclimated to the temperature swing.

Low pressure areas are a double edged sword for trout anglers. As a low approaches trout fishing is often very productive. Since we don't live in a liquid environment, pressure changes are not noticeable to us. Trout and other fish are acutely aware of pressure changes because such changes manipulate the relative pressure of the water all around them.

Think about diving into the deep end of a swimming pool. Does the water down near the bottom of the pool feel denser and does it exert more pressure on your body than the water near the surface? Sure it does, because the water at the bottom of the pool is condensed or pressurized by the weight of all the water above it pressing down. When fish move up and down in the water column the pressure changes just as it does when we jump into a pool.

On the next level let's consider a trout holding at a set depth. If the trout isn't making significant moves upward or downward in the water column does the amount of pressure they feel change? When the weather is stable and the barometric pressure is steady the pressure changes very little. When a low pressure area approaches and the barometric pressure begins to drop the relative pressure the trout feel decreases. Once the area of low press passes through the region the barometric pressure begins to push up and the relative pressure the trout feel increases.

When the relative pressure the trout feel decreases they feel more energetic and are able to move about more easily. This increased activity increases the metabolism of the trout and they feed. This in part explains why the trout fishing can be very productive as a low moves in.

When the low peaks and then begins to pass the fishing typically becomes tough. This is a direct result of the barometric pressure increasing. As the barometric pressure goes up the relative pressure the trout feel also increases. This increase makes the fish feel less energetic, they move less, their metabolism slows and they feed less.

In the simplest terms trout that are feeding are a whole lot easier to catch than those that are not feeding. A dropping barometer prompts them to feed while an increasing barometer encourages them to stop feeding. This explains why we anglers experience good fishing as a storm approaches and poor fishing after it passes.

Trout are hardwired for survival. I believe another factor in the increased feeding trout partake in as a storm approaches stems from the fact that on an instinctive level they understand that there is an upcoming period of hours or possibly even days when they will be doing very little feeding. As a result they try to pack the pantry in preparation for the lean period ahead.

Since I've never actually spoken to a trout, I'm speculating about this phenomenon, but I'm confident that this is how it works. Fish and game are very much in tune with their environments. If they weren't they could never survive and I think that the heavy feeding trout display with the approach of a storm is just an example of the instincts trout have developed helping to ensure the survival of the species.

In a perfect world we would never go fishing after an abrupt temperature drop or on the retreating edge of a low pressure area. However, in the real world most of us have to fish when we can regardless of the conditions.

This being the case, the way to deal with either a temperature drop or a retreating low is to slow down the presentation, switch to natural baits when artificials fail and use plenty of scent.

In general, the dead of winter is a great time for trout fishing. The trout are typically hungry and can be found holding near the surface, making getting a lure or bait in front of them an easy task, yet there are special challenges associated with winter fishing. Long periods of cold weather that strike during the dead of winter can drive surface temperatures down so low that rainbows and browns go into a semi-dormant state. Their metabolism and need to feed decreases greatly, they feed less and are much harder to hook as a result.

You can expect pretty good fishing until the water temperature gets into the lower 40's. Once the temperature drops below 45 I often abandon trolling and concentrate my efforts on bait fishing. When trout slow down, it is crucial to present them with a passive bait that stays in the strike zone for an extended period of time. Once again I use Pro-Cure and BioEdge at these times, since scent gives me an added edge.

Here in the Golden State it seems like we are either in a state of drought or it rains cats and dogs for weeks at a time. When we get those long periods of sustained rain during the late winter and early spring, lakes and reservoirs often become super muddy, making for tough trout fishing. For a long time I would forget fishing during such periods until the water began to clear. A few years back I stumbled on a strategy that has helped to keep me on the water during such periods of time.

While lakes can take several days or even several weeks to clear after they become clouded with mud, I've found that the streams feeding impoundments typically clear within 12 to 48 hours after the rain stops. If you motor up the arms of a muddy lake or reservoir to the area where a tributary comes in you'll often encounter an abrupt line where clear water from the tributary encounters the cloudy water of the lake. Very often this change in water clarity is stark. You can actually have muddy cloudy water on one side of the boat and clear water on the other side.

I've found that trout will often stack up around this transition zone between muddy and clear water. Since the weather is typically unstable when these conditions exist and the water is cold, trolling is not a good bet, but bait fishing can be fair to good. With all the runoff flushing into the lake worms are a natural choice.

So far we've pretty much been focused on times when the trout fishing will likely be poor as a result of the weather. Now let's explore times when the fishing is likely to be good or maybe even great. In the late 1920's a man named John Alden Knight began looking at factors that could be used to predict the daily behavior of fish and game in terms of when the highest level of activity and feeding would occur.

Without going into a long confusing explanation of Knight's findings, he determined that there are peak times of feeding and activity every day based on the location of the moon and sun. He also determined that there are some days when the activity levels and feeding behaviors of fish and game will be much more intense than they are on an average day. These are the days when we can expect the best hunting and fishing.

It took Knight about 10 years of research before he was able to perfect his system of predicting the activity and feeding levels of fish and game. Knight dubbed his findings "Solunar Tables", since his predictions were based on the interrelationship and positions of the sun and moon. For a long time I didn't put much stock in the Solunar Tables, but when I began comparing the information in my fishing journals with the predictions of the Solunar Tables I found that the tables had an uncanny ability to predict the activity levels of both fish and game and my success rate fluctuated accordingly.

The only thing that the table can't account for is the weather. For example, even if the charts predict a high level of activity, if a low is retreating during that period it will override what the tables predict and the fishing will be tough. When the tables predict minimal activity and slow fishing, an approaching low can still prompt high levels of activity and outstanding action. Having said that, when the weather is stable the tables provide a very good indication of the type of action you can expect to encounter.

There are a number of sources to obtain Solunar predictions. My favorite is Rick Taylor's Prime Times. His charts are accurate and presented in an easy to read calendar form that provides the peak feeding times and employs simple symbols to predict whether fishing and hunting will be poor, fair, good, or best on any given day.

For information or to get a copy of Taylor's predictions call (866) 809-5063 or visit them online at www.primetimes2.com.

I touched on this point earlier, but I'm going to reiterate on it in closing. This book is a guide for catching trout and catching is great. As much as we enjoy the outdoors and fresh air we are into production or we'd be bird watchers or golfers. We want our efforts to produce trout. If that weren't the case I wouldn't have written this book and you wouldn't be reading it, right?

Having said this, don't let things like temperature drops, low pressure areas and poor Solunar predictions keep you off the water. All of us are busy these days and we've got to sneak away and fish whenever we can. To quote a much repeated saying, a bad day fishing is better than the best day at work!

On another level in terms of the growth of an angler, tough bites are good. Let's face it, we don't learn much when the bite is wide open and we are catching trout after trout. It's when we have to improvise and meet the challenges of tough conditions that we become more proficient. When I go out fishing these days whether from the bank or on a boat, I'm not hoping for good conditions so I can catch fish. Everyone wants good conditions, but my mindset is that I'm going to use my experience to catch trout regardless of the conditions.

All anglers whether it's a bluegill angler fishing a pond, a tarpon guide plying the Florida Keys or a trout angler at a reservoir are all chasing the same thing. It's called consistency. We all want to catch fish consistently day in and day out. Without fishing when the conditions are poor we'll never learn how to catch trout when the going gets tough.

A day on the water when the bite is wide open is satisfying there is no doubt about it, but in a lot of ways there is even more satisfaction in using your experience and savvy to catch a handsome limit of trout when most other anglers are

struggling to get so much as a bite!

Chapter Twenty Nine: Kill And Keep Or Catch 'N' Release?

Back in our father's and grandfather's time there was never any question about what to do with the trout at the end of their line. If they were lucky enough to land it, home it went for the family table.

These days there are a lot of anglers on the water that still enjoy a good old fashion trout dinner, but there are a similar number of folks that prefer to release most of their trout to fight another day. If you put the information in this book into practice, it is likely that you'll become so proficient at catching trout that you'll never be able to eat all the fish you land. So even if you are an avid fish eater, the ability to release trout unharmed is a skill you'll need to master. Likewise, when it comes to keeping trout there are things that savvy anglers do to insure that the trout they take will provide the best possible table fare.

Before we explore how to release trout let's take a look at how to properly care for the trout you intend to keep for the table. Visit any trout lake when the fish are biting and you'll see both bank and boat anglers with trout on stringers. Trollers often tow their stringer of trout off the side of the boat, while the shore guys generally attach a short line to their stringers and toss the trout a few feet off the bank. During the dead of winter when the water is cold keeping trout on a stinger might be okay, but for the rest of the year it just doesn't work if your goal is to have the highest quality trout for the table.

The two most important things an angler can do to enhance the flavor and texture of the trout they keep is to bleed them and keep them cold. Most anglers neglect to bleed their trout and that's a mistake. If a trout isn't bled the blood that is left in the circulatory system will darken the flesh and make the meat softer. It will also impart a strong flavor to the meat.

There are a couple of different ways to bleed trout, but the simplest and most effective that I've found is to whack them on the head just hard enough to knock them out and then use a knife or scissors to cut their gills. Once the gills are cut, I immediately put the trout in a cooler. If the trout is submerged in the water melting off the ice, the meat can become waterlogged and mushy. If you're going to be out fishing for only a few hours just laying the trout on top the ice will work just fine. If you are planning to be out all day or longer, it pays to place the fish in a plastic bag once they've bled out. This way they will stay plenty cold without soaking in water.

In general, I don't like to leave the entrails in my trout for more than two or three hours. Fish have strong digestive fluids and the last thing you want these fluids to do is seep into the meat surrounding the abdominal cavity. Fortunately for us trout anglers, trout are one of the easiest game fish to clean.

Certainly you've heard the old saying that there is more than one way to skin a cat. Well, I'm here to tell you that there is more than one way to gut a trout. My favorite method is to take a razor sharp fillet knife and slit the trout open from the vent to the gills. Then I cut across the back of the trout's neck until I sever the spine. After that I set the knife aside, hold the trout's body in my left hand and pull down on the head with my right. When you pull down on the head the incision you made will continue down behind the pectoral fins, detaching the head. After the head comes off the entrails will still be attached to it. Pull downward toward the tail and all the trout's insides will come out just like that. The final step is to scrape out the blood line that lies along the spine at the top of the abdominal cavity. After that give the trout a quick rinse and the job is finished.

If you prefer to leave the head of your trout attached you still start out by slitting the trout's stomach from vent to gills. Next flare the trout's gill plates and cut the gills were they join the back of the mouth. Set the knife down and while holding the fish in you left hand, slide your right index finger through the center of the gills and down the throat. Get a firm grip on the gills and steadily pull downward toward the tail and the gills and guts will detach. Finish up by removing the bloodline followed by a good rinse.

Certain dishes call for filleted trout. Filleting is a simple task that is easily mastered with a little practice. To fillet a trout you'll need a keenly honed fillet knife. Begin by cutting downward just behind the gill plates. When you feel the spine turn the blade ninety degrees and work the knife down to the tail in one smooth deliberate sweep. When filleting trout you don't want to remove the skin from the fillet. The meat of trout is delicate and if the skin is removed the fillet will fall apart. Using most recipes the trout fillets are cooked with the skin attached and the meat is lifted off the skin just before it is eaten.

There are a lot of fish such as bass that provide boneless fillets, but with trout there remains a final step after the fillet has been removed from the trout's body. For this step you'll need a needle nose pliers or a specialized bone pulling pliers

224

often used by sushi chefs. In either case, lay the fillet on a firm surface with the skin side down. Using your index finger feel along the middle of the fillet. You'll discover a line of small stiff bones. Grab the bones with the pliers and pull them out of the fillet one at a time, using firm steady pressure.

A lot of folks are reluctant to keep trout in a cooler on multiple day trips, fearing that the fish will spoil. If you put your cleaned bagged trout in a cooler with just ice, the ice and water mixture that results will be about 32 degrees. If you take the same cooler full of ice, bury your bagged trout in the ice and then liberally sprinkle rock salt or even table salt over the ice the temperature will plummet to as low as 4 degrees. Obviously, if you salt your ice and the temperature drops below freezing there is no chance for your trout to spoil.

What is the purpose of releasing a small or unwanted fish? Now, you are probably thinking this is a silly question. Of course the purpose of releasing a fish is to put it back in the system, so it can live on to provide future fishing and a strong fishery. This being the case I'm often amazed to see how some anglers treat the fish that they release. I've seen guys grab trout in a towel, allow struggling fish to roll around in the dirt and go after hooks imbedded in a fish's throat with a pair of needle nose pliers.

Over the years I've done a good deal of fly fishing. One of the things you learn early on as a fly guy is how to properly release trout. There is a lot of controversy when it comes to netting and releasing trout. Some folks feel that a trout to be released should never be netted and there are other anglers that contend just as adamantly that netting a trout does no harm. I think both sides of this argument have merit. On one hand I believe if it is possible to land a trout that you intend to release without netting it that you should do it. However, I am aware that there are some situations where using a net is absolutely mandatory.

Trout caught while using artificial lures are nearly always hooked in the mouth and that makes releasing them easy. In most cases you can use a pliers or forceps to shake the trout off the hook without touching the fish or removing it from the water. If you need to handle the trout, wet your hands before touching it. This will help to ensure that the protective slime that coats the trout's skin won't be removed. If you touch a trout with dry hands and the slime comes off, the fish will be vulnerable to bacteria when released.

Another rule to remember when handling trout is to treat them gently. You don't want to squeeze them as this can harm their internal organs. Generally, if you cradle trout under the belly they won't struggle.

When fishing with bait, many of the trout caught will be hooked deeply. A lot of folks believe that deeply hooked trout are destined to die, but that is not the case. The worst thing an angler can do with a deeply hooked trout that they intend to release is to go after the hook with pliers. This type of "field surgery" almost always results in a bleeding highly stressed trout that has a poor chance of surviving the ordeal.

Instead of attempting to remove a deeply imbedded hook, simply cut the leader close to the trout's mouth and let the fish go. Trout and other fish have an incredible capacity to deal with foreign objects such as fish hooks. Over time the trout's body will expel the hook. After that it will either be dissolved in the body by the trout's digestive system or it will be passed out of the body via the trout's vent.

This phenomenon was driven home to me one day while I was out bass fishing. I caught a 10 inch spotted bass on a jig and as I went to release it I noticed something protruding from its vent. Taking a closer look I found that the object was a badly corroded 5/0 worm hook. I wiggled it a little and it pulled free. If that little bass could deal with that massive plastic worm hook, a trout can certainly deal with a No. 10 bait holder!

If you decide to take a picture of a trout that is going to be released, leave the fish in the water as your partner gets out the camera. When your partner is ready get the hook out of the fish or cut the leader, gently pick the fish up with wet hands and display it for the photo. After your partner squeezes off two or three shots, return the trout to the water.

Whenever you release a trout take an extra moment or two and make sure it is ready to swim on its own. At times after a prolonged fight or when a trout has been out of the water it will have a tough time swimming. When this happens, hold the trout by the tail and move it back and forth in the water, forcing water through its gills. This will invigorate the trout and when it is ready to go it will shoot out of your grasp with a burst of speed.

So there you have it, just as there is a process to catching trout, there is also a process to keeping them for the table or releasing them to fight again another day. Follow the steps in this chapter and you can look forward to many memorable trout dinners and you'll be able to release unwanted trout with confidence, knowing that they'll be just fine.

Chapter Thirty: A Picture Is Worth 1,000 Words!

In a lot of ways our lives are centered around memories and celebrating that which has passed, whether we are talking about the Baseball Hall Of Fame in Cooperstown, New York where the achievements of Babe Ruth, Joe DiMaggio and Ted

Williams are kept alive or the family photo album in the hall closet where weddings, graduations and anniversaries are recorded.

In its essence trout fishing is a here and now sport filled with challenges and adrenaline pumping excitement. But beyond this, it is an endeavor that celebrates cold mornings, warm spring afternoons, rugged scenery and the crimson stripe of a rainbow's flank. As anglers, we store these recollections deep within our minds, forming the basis for mid-week daydreams when we can't be on the water and heightening our anticipation for the next time we can partake in the sport we love.

What if we wanted to give our fishing memories a tangible quality, a physical dimension? One way to achieve this is to have your quarry preserved as a trophy mount or full size replica, but this is only a realistic option for the biggest of the big or the most meaningful trout that you catch. You're not going to call the taxidermist the next time you catch a limit of fat planter rainbows at your local lake, despite the fact that the experience was thoroughly enjoyable. While such an achievement falls far short of demanding a visit to the taxidermist, it is a still an event worthy of some level of preservation. In other words it's time to break out the camera!

As a longtime freelance writer and a full time editor at the Fish Sniffer Magazine, part of my job is taking photos of successful anglers and evaluating photos taken by others. In the course of a year I probably snap off in excess of a thousand photos and view several thousand more. With this level of hands on experience and exposure it doesn't take long to determine what makes for a good photograph and what factors add up to make a bad one.

Taking a good photo depends on preparation and forethought. A lot of folks believe that to take a good photo you've got to have an expensive, top of the line camera. In reality a great fishing photo can be taken with an inexpensive disposable camera just as easily as it can be taken with a sophisticated digital camera.

Before we consider what goes into a good photo let's take a look at some of the common errors photographers make that consistently result in poor pictures. Movement and poor lighting are a photographer's worst enemies. If you move the camera as the shot is taken, the photo is going to come out fuzzy. To have tack sharp photos you don't need to shoot off a tripod. If you shoot rifles or handguns, you've got a good idea of how to snap off a photo without movement.

The first thing you want to do is position your feet apart to establish a firm base or drop down to one knee. Next get a firm grasp on the camera with both hands. Line the subject up in the view finder, take a deep breath, let half of it out and then gently squeeze off the photo moving only the tip of your finger. When the shutter snaps stay statue still for a moment or two. I often find myself anticipating the shutter when taking a series of photos and moving before it has actually closed and captured the image. By focusing on remaining still until I'm sure I've got the shot, I have a lot less fuzzy photos.

Poor lighting results in shadows and of course shadows result in dark spots within photographs. The first step in eliminating shadows is to always set up with the sun on the photographer's back and make sure that the photographer's shadow is not being cast onto the subject. Early and late in the day are among the best times to take quality photos because the sun is low in the sky and illuminates the subject from the front.

At high noon taking a good shot can be difficult because illumination is coming from above. I see a frustrating number of photos that look great except for one thing, the sun is high in the sky and the subject's baseball hat is casting a dark shadow right over their face. In pictures like these the fish invariably looks wonderful, but the angler's face is completely blacked out. If you have to take a photo when the sun is high make sure to have the subject remove or tilt back their hat, or retreat into an area that features complete shade and use the camera's flash for illumination. Speaking of flash, you should always use the flash when taking a fishing photo regardless of the lighting conditions. This will go a long way toward eliminating small shadows that take away from the quality of any photo.

Another factor that greatly affects the quality and visual impact of a photograph is the distance or apparent distance that the camera is from the subject. Remember the object of a fishing portrait is to showcase the angler showing off their catch. That means you want to be up close and you want the subject to fill up the frame as much as possible without cutting off any part of the angler's head or the fish's body. I see a lot of well set up photos where the subject only occupies between twenty five and fifty percent of the frame.

When I set up to take a portrait I take three or four shots at super close range, really testing the limits of the frame. I then back off a touch and take three or four more just in case I cut off a bit of the fish or angler in the first four shots. As you shoot, alternate the camera from a horizontal position to a vertical position. This will add variety to your photo collection.

This raises another important point. Don't be stingy with shots. I might take eight photos of a subject and seven of them will be good, but in one of them the subject will have that special glint in their eye and that picture turns out to be head and shoulders better than the rest.

So how do you set up a good fishing portrait? First of all don't lose sight of the fact that the photographer is the equivalent of a movie director, meaning that you've got to take charge and direct the action. The best time to take trout fishing portrait is right after the trout is caught, before it's colors fade and it loses its life like luster. The person that caught the trout is going to be excited and will want to get their line back into the water, but be assertive and get your shots.

As you set up the shot make sure the fish is clean of blood, sand, leaves or other debris. Have the subject display the trout such that all or most of their hand is behind the fish. You want the angler to display the fish out in front of their body and just below their face. You don't want the fish down around their waist, but you don't want it blocking out the subject's face either. Before you shoot the photo look at the subject's elbows. When people display fish they have a tendency to stick their elbows out the sides of their body and they end up looking unnatural. Remind them to pull their elbows in line with their forearms. As you thumb through fishing magazines take note of the pictures and remember how the anglers display their fish and try to incorporate what you observe into your own photos.

As important as the lighting and how the subject displays the trout is, the setting and background of the photo are just as important. In terms of setting, you can take a fair photo at the boat ramp or in your backyard, but to take a great photo you've got to be on the bank or out on the water where the action actually took place.

When I talk about the background, I'm thinking about the clothing the angler is wearing, since that is what will be directly behind the trout, but I'm also thinking about how the angler's clothing will stand out against the surrounding terrain.

In general you want to wear brightly colored clothing that will contrast greatly with the trout and the terrain. Reds, blues and yellows are among the best colors while white, black and camouflage are the worst. White stands out against most natural terrain, but trout don't show up well against white. The opposite is true of black. Trout show up good against it, but it doesn't work well with most natural backgrounds. Camouflage is a double whammy, since it blends in against natural backgrounds and fish blend into it. In this way contrast is lost and a poor photo is often the result.

As a final thought about the background, having the sky visible at the top of a photograph can really enhance its overall appearance. To capture the subject, the woods or water and the sky all in one frame the best strategy is to kneel down slightly lower than your subject and shoot at an upward angle.

The End

I hope you enjoyed the book as much as I enjoyed the research (fishing!) that went into writing it. Be on the lookout for other books in the works as well as reading our "Fish Sniffer" Magazine.

www.fishsniffer.com

Cal Kellogg

www.ingramcontent.com/pod-product-compliance
Lightning Source LLC
Chambersburg PA
CBHW071419090426
42737CB00011B/1513